The National Consumer Law Center

 GUIDE TO

Mobile Homes

a.k.a. MANUFACTURED HOMES

D0913842

Selected Other
National Consumer Law Center
Publications
(see pages 117 to 123 for a complete list)

The National Consumer Law Center Guide to
Surviving Debt

The National Consumer Law Center Guide to
Consumer Rights for Immigrants

Return to Sender: Getting a Refund or Replacement
for Your Lemon Car

Consumer Warranty Law

Stop Predatory Lending

The National Consumer Law Center

GUIDE TO

Mobile Homes

a.k.a. MANUFACTURED HOMES

Bill J. White

National Consumer Law Center
Boston MA
www.consumerlaw.org

For reprint permission or ordering information, contact:
Publications Department, NCLC, 77 Summer St., 10th Fl., Boston, MA 02110-1006
(617) 542-9595, Fax (617) 542-8028,
E-mail publications@nclc.org
www.consumerlaw.org

Library of Congress Control No. 2002101892
ISBN 1-931697-17-5

10 9 8 7 6 5 4 3 2 1

This book contains suggestions and advice for those considering the purchase of a manufactured (mobile) home. The contents do not represent interpretations of state or federal laws nor does it contain legal advice. The reader is strongly urged to consult legal counsel regarding any concern they may have about the contracts and agreements involved in the purchase or financing of a manufactured home.

Cover design and illustration by Lightbourne, copyright © 2002.
Inside Photographs, NCLC copyright ©2002.

ABOUT THE AUTHOR

Bill J. White is Chief Inspector and Principal Owner of Interstate Inspection Services, Benton, Arkansas. He conducts inspections of mobile (manufactured) homes for defects in their construction, installation, or for transportation or storm damage. Mr. White was former Inspector and Inspector Supervisor at the Arkansas Manufactured Home Commission, a state agency, from 1988 to 1997.

ACKNOWLEDGMENTS

My sincere thanks to Mary Beth Bowman for her assistance in compiling this publication. Special thanks to Roger S., Jack M., Ralph C., Jim B., John J., Mike R., Jerry S., Mike M., Jack P., Ed S., Rick W., and "Dead-eye" Don K., for sharing with me their experiences, knowledge, expertise, and good humor while on the road in search of the perfect "0 points" mobile home factory.

Thanks also to Denise Lisio for editing the manuscript and compiling the appendices and glossary; Dorothy Tan for editorial assistance; Ani Tashjian, Ani Design Associates, for typesetting; and Mary McLean for indexing.

This book is dedicated
to my wife Hazel.

CONTENTS

PREFACE

About one-third of all new homes sold in this country are manufactured homes, commonly called "mobile homes." In this book the term "mobile home" will be used for the sake of brevity and because most dealers advertise and sell such homes using that terminology. The term applies to all single-section and multi-sectional homes that are labeled to comply with the standards established by HUD after passage of the National Manufactured Home Construction and Safety Standards Act of 1974. The standards are commonly called the HUD Code.

For over nine years I have reviewed thousands of formal complaints submitted to the Arkansas Manufactured Home Commission by mobile home buyers and listened to thousands of other complaints that were called in to the agency by telephone. The majority of those complaints involved one or more of five basic concerns. The number one complaint concerned mobile homes that were defectively designed and/or defectively constructed. The next most common complaint was that the home was not properly installed. Damage to the home during transportation to the home site was the third most common complaint. The fourth most common complaint was that the buyer had, in some manner, been defrauded or deceived by the dealer or salesperson. The fifth most common complaint was that factory warranty service could not be obtained, or if warranty work had been done it was done sloppily or ineffectively.

Keep in mind, there are many honest, hardworking manufactured home dealers and salespeople. There are others who are out to "rip your head off" by using misrepresentations and misinformation to sell you a low-end home at an inflated price. ("I ripped their heads off" is a term which is often used by shyster mobile home salespersons when bragging to others in the business about having sold a mobile home for *substantially* more than it was worth.)

There are some well designed and well built, energy efficient, mobile homes on dealers' lots across the country, but there are also too many badly designed, poorly constructed, and minimally insulated homes that will self destruct in a few years, costing the buyer an arm and a leg in heating and cooling expenses while doing it.

The hardest pill for a home buyer to swallow is that after spending big bucks to find and purchase a good, solid, well built and insulated home at a fair price, they realize months later the home was defectively installed and has sustained structural damage as a result of the shoddy installation.

Most mobile home buyers do not have the income or resources to purchase a site-built home. Neither do most mobile home buyers have the resources to obtain legal counsel when they have been ripped-off by a dealer, installer or manufacturer. The purpose of this book is to assist those buyers in obtaining the best mobile home for their money and avoiding the problems that often arise from the purchase. A lot of the tips and suggestions contained in the book are derived from the experiences of thousands of mobile home buyers who believed they "got their heads ripped off" when they bought their homes. The rest of the tips and suggestions come from my experiences as a mobile home salesman, a factory warranty serviceman, as a mobile home inspector for both a state agency and HUD, and from six decades of classes in the school of hard knocks.

This book is not intended to portray the industry as a whole in a bad light. It is intended to help steer unsuspecting home buyers away from the people and products that have themselves given the industry a black eye.

The manufactured home industry will, of course, be highly critical of this book. Their well-oiled propaganda machines will begin chattering at high speed when the book is printed. And that's OK, it's the propagandist's and lobbyist's job to keep the industry's image polished, even those parts that need sand blasting first.

A few things you as a manufactured home buyer should keep in mind. The people who buy manufactured (mobile) homes pay, *very directly*, the salaries and wages of every person employed by HUD's Manufactured Home Division and the salaries of all the states' Manufacturer Home Agencies' and Commissions' staff. The home's costs to the buyers also pay the salaries and wages of everyone else making a living from this industry, including the Design Approval and Inspection agencies. Your purchase also funds the industry's state and national trade associations.

When you buy a new mobile home, the price will include a "HUD Label Fee" which goes to HUD, who in turn pays the state agencies to handle and resolve consumer complaints regarding mobile homes. In the contract the state agencies have with HUD to handle consumer complaints, there is a requirement the agencies not be stacked with industry representatives who might take control of the agency's functions.

Very unfortunately for the home buyers in many states, the state agencies (called State Administrative Agencies in the federal regulations) have been dominated and controlled by the industry for many years. That control has been so obvious that HUD officially notified some agencies a few years ago that their regulatory activities were in violation of the Federal Manufactured Home Procedural and Enforcement Regulations and in violation of the agencies' contract with HUD. After a lot of bureaucratic paper shuffling, little has been done to regain control of those agencies from the industry. In a lot of states, especially in the South, it is still a case of the fox guarding the henhouse.

Included in the cost to the new home buyer in many states is a fee of from $50 to $100 which goes directly to the private industry associations. That money pays the salary of the Association's lobbyist, propagandist, and staff, and is doled out as needed between the local politicians and the Washington politicians to serve the purpose and interests of the industry.

The reason for expanding upon the somewhat maternal ties between the industry and the agencies which superficially regulate it is this: You, as a mobile home buyer, are pretty much on your own. There may be no agency in your state government that is actually going to stand up to the industry on your behalf if you are a mobile home buyer that has had "your head ripped off." Be careful out there.

I am not an attorney and do not intend to give you legal advice, but common sense advice. I do highly recommend that any person asked to sign any kind of purchase agreement or retail installment contract which contains conditions or terms that they are uncomfortable with, or do not fully understand, take the unsigned documents to an attorney of their choice for review and clarification. The fee an attorney will charge for the service will be small in comparison to what you may stand to loose. The review of the documents by an attorney should give you some confidence and security in making your decision about the transaction.

INTRODUCTION

If you purchase a mobile home because you believe, for any reason, that it is "built just like a site built home and to the same standards," you will most likely be disappointed with the home you buy. Mobile homes are designed and intended to be "affordable housing." The price of a new mobile home is very substantially less than the cost of a home built on site to meet a recognized building code. The reason for the difference in the cost of site built homes and manufactured homes should be obvious to anyone who has closely inspected both.

There are very few modular homes sold by mobile home dealers in the South and Southwest. There are many sold elsewhere. Modular homes are expensive to build and expensive to install.

Modular homes are built to nationally recognized building codes; mobile home are built to the HUD Code, which is quite different. Modular homes are built on a temporary metal frame which is returned to the factory after the home is set on its foundation. The metal frame of a mobile home can not, by federal law, be removed. (If it were removed, the floor framing system of most mobile homes would probably deform or overturn under the home's weight when set on a foundation.)

This is how you tell the difference: if the home or section has a little, red HUD label on the tail-light end, it's a mobile home, regardless of what a salesperson tells you. And when a mobile home salesperson, or anyone else, tells you that mobile homes are built "just like site-built homes," you can take it to the bank that person is either as ignorant as a pine cone or lying like a yard dog.

The tag is aluminum, painted red, and has an identification number stamped into the metal. The ID number consists of a three letter prefix and six or seven digits. The reason for this boring description of the HUD label is that sometimes mobile home salespersons or dealers will tell a potential buyer that the multi-section homes on the dealer's lot are "modular" homes instead of manufactured (mobile)

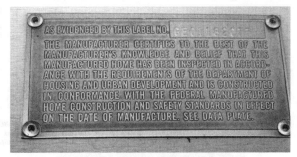

A HUD label showing the State of Georgia as the Primary Inspection Agency in the plant where the home was produced

homes. This deception is a relatively common complaint and may, at best, be only the result of ignorance on the speaker's part. If the deception is intentional, it is fraudulent misrepresentation of a product. "Modular" and "manufactured" (mobile) homes are definitely not the same.

While on the subject of HUD labels, modular homes, and the HUD Code, one more thing needs to be clarified. Since 1974 the U.S. Department of Housing and Urban Development (HUD) has had the responsibility of establishing and updating construction and safety standards for all manufactured (mobile) homes sold in this country (even if manufactured in another country) and the responsibility to monitor each manufacturer's compliance with those standards. Each manufacturer must attach a metal tag to the tail-light end of each home, or to each section of a multi-sectional home, which basically certifies that the manufacturer *believes* the home complies with the requirements of the HUD Construction and Safety Standards that were in effect at the time the home was built.

The inspections of manufactured homes on the production lines are not done by HUD inspectors. (Some salespeople tell anyone who will listen that "HUD inspects every one of our homes.") Not so. In most states in which mobile homes are produced those inspections are done by private inspection agencies. A few states actually do the in-plant inspections. The three letters that make up the first part of the HUD label number denote which agency inspects the homes on a particular manufacturer's production line. As is evident from the number of defective homes built and sold, it is clear some of the inspection agencies, both state and private, are doing a very lousy job.

— 1 —

DEALING WITH DEALERS AND SALESPEOPLE

A mobile home will probably be the most expensive purchase most buyers will ever make. Some multi-section homes sold in the South and Southwest may have a price tag of over $70,000. In the Western states the price might be over $200,000. With interest on a long term loan, the cost to you will more than double. That's why you should very carefully shop and compare before signing on the dotted line. To help you in doing that, you should consider the following advice.

(1) *Never deal with high-pressure salespeople who insist that you give them personal information or complete and sign a credit application as soon as you set foot on their lot.*

Some of the larger dealerships have very high-pressure sales tactics and questionable advertising that are designed to "lure and lock you in" the first time you set foot on their lot. They want your credit report before they get off their backsides to show you any home. If they find you have good credit, the rush is on. Be *very* wary on such lots. Most mobile home salespeople work on commission and the business is very competitive. The salesperson's commission is usually a percentage of the sales price of the home. Often a home is sold at an outlandishly inflated price to an unwary buyer so that a greedy salesperson can make a few hundred dollars more in commission.

(2) *Never deal with a salesperson who misleads you about the features of any home.*

The most common misrepresentations made by mobile home salespersons are discussed below:

(a) You are told the floors are "all tongue & groove plywood" when they may in fact be particle board or oriented strand board (OSB) with square edges.

Check the decking yourself. If it's a multi-section home, lift the carpet at the marriage line (where the sections meet when joined) and look at the decking. If it's a single-wide, ask the salesperson to have one of the heat registers in the floor removed so you can look at the edges of the floor decking in the floor opening. (Some manufacturers place the conditioned air ducts in the ceiling and its difficult to find a way to see the floor decking.)

(b) You are told wall, floor, and roof framing is "all on 16" centers" when in fact some or all of the framing may be spaced 24" on center.

Check the spacing of the wall studs by measuring the spacing of the interior wallboard fasteners. (Look for the line of fastener holes in the wallboard. The HUD Code requires the wallboard be fastened to every stud.)

TIP **All U.S. paper currency is exactly 6" long. If it is less than three bill lengths between framing members, they are 16" on center. If four bill lengths apart, the framing is 24" on center.**

Check the spacing of the floor joists by feeling along the underneath side of the home below the outside walls. You can feel the ends of the floor joists through the bottom board material (the black plastic material under the floor) and measure the distance between them.

You will not be able to check the spacing of the trusses in a single-wide home on a dealer's lot. If multi-section homes are not joined closely together on the sales lot, you may be able to see the trusses from the ground, even through the plastic sheeting that is usually covering the opening into the attic cavity.

(c) You are told the roof rafters are 2" X 4"'s (or 2" X 6"'s) when the roof framing is actually trusses made from 2" X 2" (actual dimensions are closer to 1-1/4" X 1-1/2") lumber.

Most homes sold in the Southern half of the country, and many in other parts of the country have 2" X 2" roof trusses.

(d) You are told the roof cavity, floor cavity, and wall cavity have "upgraded insulation" when the cavities may in fact be insulated with the bare minimum allowed by the HUD Code's Thermal Design requirements.

Federal law requires that each manufacturer furnish an Insulation Disclosure Form that shows the actual insulation used in each home. You have the right to see that form before purchase.

(3) *Never deal with a salesperson who offers to include false credit information or false information about the amount of the down payment on the loan application to help you obtain a home loan.*

Submitting false information on a credit application is a violation of the law. If you conspire with the salesperson to file such false information, you are at that person's mercy, and stand to lose your home if the finance company discovers the deception. You may also be subject to criminal prosecution.

(4) *Never accept a salesperson's word that only one source of financing is available for the homes sold from that lot.*

Most dealerships have several sources of financing. FHA and VA financing with lower interest rates may be available, but the salesperson may not make you aware of that because there is more paperwork involved and it will take a little longer to complete the sales transaction. Many salespeople would rather arrange conventional financing which is less work for them, although it may cost you thousands of dollars in additional interest. FHA or VA insured loans may be two percentage points lower than conventional loans. The total interest on a 20-year loan of $25,000 at 8% is $25,184; the interest at 10% would be $32,900. That's a difference of $7,716. (The total amount you will pay in premium and interest for a loan of $25,000 at 10% for 20 years will be $57,900. The same $25,00 loan at 8% will result in total interest and premium of $50,184.)

Many local banks and mortgage companies offer mobile home loans at lower interest rates, especially if you own, or are buying, the land on which the mobile home is to be placed.

(5) *Never agree to purchase a specially ordered home from the factory unless* **all** *of the special options and features that you want are shown on the* **Purchase Agreement**, *along with the price of each option or feature.*

TIP Before you buy, get a copy of the sales brochures that the manufacturer supplies the dealer which contain the floor plan and the "standard features" list for the home you are interested in buying. It may show the spacing and size of structural components, insulation values, and types and qualities of other materials and components used in the home. If the "standard features" list does not show the spacing of floor, wall, and framing members, they are likely on 24" center. If the type of floor decking used is not shown to be plywood or OSB (oriented strand board), it is likely particle board. If the floor decking used is described by a trade name, it is likely particle board. (One type of floor decking commonly used in mobile homes is particle board sold under the trade name of Novadeck™.)

Also ask the dealer or salesman to provide you with a copy of the purchase order sent to the manufacturer for the home you are ordering. Double check to see that the salesperson has listed on the order the features that are on the purchase agreement.

Also make sure that purchase agreement shows the *TOTAL* purchase price, including options, delivery, installation, and air conditioning and skirting, if included in the sales price.

Something to watch out for: Some dealers show "Skirting Included" in their advertisements and use that wording on the purchase agreement. Only after all the loan papers have been signed, the home delivered, and after the dealer has gotten his money from the loan company, does the buyer find out that the installation of the skirting was not included in the deal. The dealer simply has someone bring boxes of skirting to your home and dump it in your yard.

Another thing to watch out for: When a dealer's ads and purchase agreements say "Air Conditioning Included," it usually does not specify what size air conditioning unit is to be installed. Be sure the size air conditioner the dealer intends to use for your home is large enough to cool it without the unit running day and night in hot weather.

TIP   **Never, under any circumstances, sign a purchase agreement or any other document or form that is blank or incompletely filled out, and never agree to sign a new purchase agreement unless everything is the same as the original one except for mutually agreed on changes.**

(6) *Always negotiate for the best price.*

The asking price usually includes allowances for delivery and set-up of the home in any part of your state or area. It will also usually include some "bargaining room." Negotiate for the bottom dollar price, especially if your home site is close to the dealer's lot and the site is reasonably level and readily accessible. (It costs the dealer more in labor and materials to install a home back in the boondocks on a steep hill than on a flat lot in a mobile home park that is located a mile from the sales lot.)

(7) *Never pay any attention to an advertisement that says "FREE AIR CONDITIONING," "FREE SKIRTING" or "FREE SET-UP AND DELIVERY." There "ain't no such animals" as free air conditioners, free skirting, or free installations. If you get them in the deal, you are going to pay for them. Period.*

(8) *Never purchase a new home that has been significantly damaged in transit to the dealer lot.*

It is a violation of federal regulations (and some states' regulations) for a dealer to sell a new manufactured home that is damaged or defective.

(9) *Never buy a home on the dealers lot in which the appliances must be changed from gas to electric, or electric to gas to meet your needs.*

The dealer is permitted under federal regulations to make such alterations, although in most of the altered homes I have inspected, the alterations resulted in the homes being brought out of conformance with the HUD Code. In many cases, the defects introduced by the alterations involved fire safety or electrical requirements.

(10) *If you are paying cash for a mobile home,* **never pay the full amount to the dealer until all the goods and services you have agreed to buy have been delivered to you!**

In most states the home's set-up and anchoring is nearly always a part of the purchase price. Also, in most cases, an installed air conditioning unit is a part of the purchase price. At times, skirting, steps, poured concrete footings, furniture, or custom built decks are include in the sales agreements.

If you have paid the dealer the full cash price before the home has left his lot, he will have no incentive to get the home delivered and set-up or to deliver the other options you purchased. The other homes he has sold which are being financed will likely have first priority when he is scheduling deliveries and installations. He has to deliver those homes before he can get his money from the loan company, but he will already have your money in his pocket.

Of the hundreds of people who have called me to complain about the time delays in getting delivery of their homes after paying the full cash price in advance, nearly all of them stated emphatically; "My biggest mistake was that I paid the dealer the full price while the home was still on the dealer's lot."

Not long ago, there was a dealer in the northeastern part of Arkansas that went out of business without furnishing air conditioners to buyers who had already paid for them. The good news is, that guy has not yet opened another sales lot. The bad news is, he probably will. He always manages somehow to get back into the business.

When paying cash for a mobile home, take the advice of people who have done it; always keep in reserve (in an escrow account if necessary) at least 20%

of the purchase price until the home is properly installed and all other goods and services shown on the purchase agreement have been delivered to you.

And a few special notes: Even though you may be paying in cash, you should still have a signed, itemized purchase agreement. You can request that the purchase agreement show that you will pay a portion of the money before the home is delivered and the rest after it has been delivered and all the other goods and services delivered to you. If the dealer refuses to accept the deal under those conditions, find a dealer that will.

(11) *Always read carefully the front **and back** of the purchase agreement before you sign it.*

The purchase agreement will likely be the first document you will be asked to sign after you have agreed to purchase a home. The form will usually have multiple, duplicate pages, and have the dealer's name and address printed at the top. The top section describes the home your are buying. The lower portion is divided into two vertical columns.

On the left side will be a list of the options, features, equipment, or services that are to be included in the deal, along with the costs for each, if they are broken out. Sometimes the form will simply show "Included" instead of the actual costs to you for air conditioning, skirting, or other materials.

The right side column shows a summary of the price, taxes, down payment, fees, and other costs.

TIP **Although you will be asked to sign only the front side of this form, there are conditions printed on the back side of the form which become a part of the agreement when it is signed.**

Even though the delivery and installation of the home is included in the price of the home, the conditions usually printed on the *back* of the purchase agreement make you responsible for the costs of a dozer or wrecker if one is needed to put the home on site.

Insist that the dealer have a competent person look at your selected home site before a purchase agreement is signed if there is any question about whether or not the home you want can be put on site and whether or not a wrecker or dozer will be required.

Another provision now frequently found on the back page of some purchase agreements prevents you from filing a lawsuit against the dealer, manufacturer or lender for any reason. Provisions in the agreement require you to have any conflict or disagreement with the parties resolved by arbitration rather than by the courts. You will usually have to pay the costs of having your case arbitrated, whatever that might be. That same provision is now contained in some finance companies' Retail Installment Contract Agreements. You may wish to have any purchase agreement or retail installment contract reviewed by an attorney before you sign them. If the dealer will not allow you to have these documents reviewed by an attorney before you sign them, look for a dealer that will. (Many dealers will not allow the consumer to take the unsigned sales or loan documents, or copies of them, from the sales lot.)

(12) *If at all possible you should not allow furniture, additional appliances, or premiums for the initial year's insurance on the home to be included in the sales price and the retail installment (financing) contract.*

The interest you will pay to have those items included in the contact will more than double their cost to you.

One last tip about dealing with salespeople: Some of the terms you make hear from salespeople have no real meaning or significance to you when trying to evaluate the quality of a home or its components. Some examples are:

(a) "This home is *the top of the line.*" (It may be the best that particular manufacturer or dealer has to offer and still be a "low-end" product with few redeeming values or features.)

(b) "The home has *upgrade carpet.*" (The standard carpet the manufacturer uses may be as thin as a bath towel; the "upgrade" may be as thick as a beach towel.)

This would be "Upgrade" carpeting in some brands of manufactured homes

(c) "We sell *factory direct.*" (99% of the new homes on dealers' lots come directly from a manufacturing plant.)

WHAT TO LOOK FOR
IN A NEW HOME

The fact that a manufacturer has placed a HUD label on the tail-light end of a mobile home which says the manufacturer *believes* it was built to meet the HUD Code doesn't mean the home is free of defects.

There are some plants throughout the country that have exceptionally good Quality Assurance (QA) programs which prevent "lemons" from being shipped to dealers. (HUD requires all plants to have effective QA programs.) There are other plants that have QA programs that are very ineffective, and the presence of a HUD label on a home from one of those plants doesn't mean much.

It will be difficult for you to see the differences in the quality of the various homes on dealers' lot until you have looked closely at a few of them. One thing in your favor is that you will usually be able to spot the clunkers if you look closely. The thing you should keep in mind is this: If the portions of the home that *you can see* are shoddily assembled and display a noticeable lack of workmanship, you can bet the parts *you can't see* are going to be as bad or worse. (If it looks like a duck and quacks like a duck, rest assured it's not a swan.)

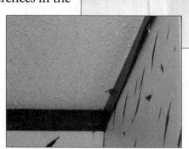

Defectively fastened wall trim

To help you in finding the better quality homes, let's start with some fundamental advice.

> *Never buy a home because it is advertised as the lowest priced home in the area or because the monthly payments will be the lowest you will find. Two quick examples:*

One large dealership special ordered all of its display units to be built as cheaply as the HUD Code would allow, *i.e.*, all framing on 24" center, particle board flooring, R-7 insulation in the walls and sub-floor, R-11 insulation in the attic, cheap doors, fixtures, appliances, etc. The dealer advertised and sold the homes based on their low price and low monthly payments. What shocked the buyers who did not inquire about the home's insulation beforehand was the fact their monthly heating and cooling bills exceeded their house payment.

Another dealer bought some *really low end* single-wide homes from a new plant that had just opened in a southeastern state. The selling price of the homes was advertised to be unbelievably low. He ran the ads before he actually received the first homes. The advertised price was so low that I decided to take a look at some of the first to arrive. I was privileged to see the lowest priced home sold in Arkansas in modern times, although it had somewhat self-destructed on its journey from the plant to central Arkansas. The condition of the home upon its arrival was so noteworthy as to merit special correspondence to the manufacturer and to HUD in Washington.

You should think twice, or nine times, before buying a home that has any of the features or conditions described below.

(a) *A very loose or wrinkled metal roof, or one that appears to be tightly stretched on a hot and sunny day.*

An unusually loose or wrinkled metal roof most likely has cracks in the galvanized coating which will cause the underlying metal to rust prematurely. If unusually loose, the metal may have flexed and split during the home's delivery to the dealer's lot from the factory. Loose roof metal produces excessive "roof rumble" in even moderate winds. If a metal roof is tightly

A defective lap joint in a two-piece metal roof

One of four holes in a metal roof that flexed and cracked during transit

stretched when installed in hot weather, the contraction of the metal in cold weather will cause the seams to loosen and the metal to be stressed at the fastener locations along the sidewalls. Metal roofs that are stretched tightly also produce excessive rumble when one side of the home faces the local prevailing winds.

(b) *A shingled roof that has ridges or noticeable dips in the roof surface.*

That one needs no explanation.

(c) *A shingled roof which has broken, misaligned, or missing shingles.*

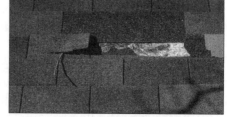

A broken shingle that allowed damage to the roof/ceiling system

There may already be leaks in the roof as the home sits on the dealer's lot.

(d) *Sagging or cracked ceilings, or ceilings with unusually high ridges at the mudded joints between the ceiling board panels.*

The need to avoid a home with sagging or cracked ceilings needs no explanation. Excessive texturing ("mud") over the joints in the ceiling board panels will nearly always crack, and sometimes fall loose, within a few months.

(e) *Loose or broken wallboard panels.*

Wallboard panels should not loosen in transit if properly fastened and if the home is properly designed. If the home left the plant with inadequately fastened wallboard panels, it means a thorough, final-finish Quality Assurance inspection was not done. So what else did they miss?

(f) *Vinyl siding that is fastened tightly to the sheathing underneath it, or vinyl siding that is unusually warped and bowed, or not well fitted around windows and doors.*

Vinyl siding not properly fastened or lapped

Vinyl siding not properly fastened. Note wavy appearance

Vinyl siding that is fastened tightly to the underlying sheathing will warp and bow with temperature changes. It is required to be loosely fastened to expand and contract during changes in outside temperature without warping. If any part of the underlying sheathing is exposed, the vinyl is not properly installed. If joints are not lapped at least 1", the vinyl is not properly installed. If any part of the installation of the vinyl allows water to contact the sheathing behind it, the vinyl is not properly installed.

TIP The vinyl siding installed on manufacturer homes is not as thick (or as expensive) as that normally used on site-built homes. That is why it warps and bows if it is not properly fastened.

(g) *A metal roof **and** exterior hardboard siding.*

Hardboard siding was never meant to be installed on any home in a manner or location that allows rainwater to routinely run over its surface. The use of hardboard siding on metal roofed mobile homes has caused expensive nightmares for tens of thousands of mobile home buyers. HUD has been asked numerous times to prohibit the use of hardboard siding under conditions it was never designed to withstand, but HUD has not done so. As in other such cases, the home buyers themselves have recently addressed the problem by filing class action lawsuits against the manufacturers of the hardboard siding materials.

(h) *A shingle roof with less than 6" overhang.*

Rainwater will sheet down the side of the home leading to rot.

(i) *Flimsy kitchen cabinets with 1" X 1" framing or shelves made of wall paneling.*

Some manufacturers use 1" X 1" strips (actually 3/4" X 3/4") for cabinet framing and thin wood paneling for shelving. As would be expected, the materials will not support the normal loads of kitchenware and utensils.

A main frame I-beam that was damaged during the home's installation

(j) *A metal frame that is drooping over the wheel and axles.*

A frame that is sagging is either too weak to support the weight of the home in transit or it has been damaged in transit. In either case, don't make it your problem. (Sometimes manufacturers will build a special model home with log siding and fail to take the added weight into account when the frame is designed and built.)

(k) *Metal siding that is wrinkled or torn at the screw hole locations.*

Damaged metal siding is an indication that the metal frame is weak or was damaged in transit. If the frame flexes abnormally in transit, the movement of the outside walls of the home will cause the screws to shear through the metal siding.

Metal siding damaged in transit

(l) *Large holes in the bottom board material (the black plastic sheeting under the floor).*

Plastic bottom board and sub-floor insulation cut and gaped. Underside of floor exposed

Believe it or not, the black, plastic sheeting under the home (called the "bottom board" in the HUD Code and called the "belly board" by others) is the air infiltration barrier for the underside of the home. It is also the rodent barrier. Any openings in the material will allow air to pour into the sub-floor cavity and into the living space through the holes in the floor decking underneath tubs, showers, and sinks. The openings will also provide easy access for mice and rats, and in one case reported to me, a large black snake.

Duct tape is not a suitable or an approved patch material for the bottom board. If you see duct tape covering large areas of the bottom board don't spend any more time looking at that home. Large areas of patches in the bottom board usually means there have been major repairs to the floor system or other systems or components inside the sub-floor cavity.

Floor decking loose because nails missed the floor joist

(m) *Loose floor decking or decking edges that show through the vinyl floor covering.*

The decking is either improperly fastened to the joists, or the joints were not sanded, or the floor system has sustained transit damage. Let the dealer and manufacturer sort it out on the dealer's lot, not on yours.

(n) *Less than 3-1/2" (R-11) insulation in the exterior walls, less than 5-1/2" (R-22) in the roof, or less than R-11 under the floor. (If a home has 2" X 6" exterior walls, the insulation in the walls can be increased to a thickness of 5-1/2" (R-19).)*

In the northern parts of the country the attic insulation should be increased to the maximum extent possible as long as the insulation can be evenly distributed over the entire attic and still maintain clearance for attic ventilation.

The trusses used in many manufactured homes, especially in some of the "low-end" homes built in the South and Southeast, will not allow a thick layer of evenly distributed attic insulation near the sidewalls. There just is not space available to install it and still maintain the required clearance for attic ventilation. But that will not stop the dealer and manufacturer from selling you more attic insulation than can be properly distributed. The insulation that can't be put along the sides of the attic will be heaped in the areas of the attic that have more space. Its done daily, and HUD and the inspectors know it, and design approval agencies allow it.

Inadequate insulation in the sub-floor, walls, and ceiling will always result in high utility bills. Ordering upgrade insulation will more than pay for the initial costs by reducing the cost of the energy used to heat and cool the home. Of course, you can't upgrade the insulation in a home after its built without great expense.

(o) *A water supply system that does not have shut-off valves at every fixture.*

When you have to change faucets or faucet washers, or work on the commode, you can do so without turning off the water to the entire house. The shut-off valves are not required by the HUD Code and they may have to be special ordered when the home is built. Some manufacturers, bless their souls, install the valves as a standard feature in their homes, but not many of them do. (Many times, just for the heck of it, I have asked manufacturers' production staff why the plant did not put shut off valves at each fixture. They usually responded by saying it would cost them 10 or 20 extra dollars per house. Big deal! One plant foreman actually told me they would have to get special approval from HUD to do it! Of course that was untrue.)

(p) *A home with a 20 gallon water heater.*

The reason for that one should be obvious to a person with a family.

(q) *A home with a large hydro-massage tub and a 20 or 30 gallon water heater.*

Would you believe some manufacturers install a small water heaters as a standard feature and do not increase the size even when a large hydro-massage tub is special ordered? Unless the water temperature on the heater is set high enough to scald a hog, the large tubs can't be filled above the jets with warm water!

(r) *A home that has shower heads over bath tubs with the shower walls made with vinyl covered sheet rock or cellulose wallboard and with batten trim covering the corner joints.*

A few manufacturers still throw together such tub/shower compartment walls. The sloppy methods used in the design and assembly of the walls allow water leakage into the substrate of the wall panels and into the corner joints, rotting both the wall board, wall framing and floor decking in the immediate vicinity.

INSPECTING YOUR HOME

TIP A note on inspection: Spend time looking over every aspect of the home. In the long run, the time you spend is money in the bank.

You should *closely inspect* a home from one end to the other, both from the inside and outside. The majority of the individual complaint items on the lists submitted to the state agencies by disgruntled home owners involve common factory defects in a home's interior or exterior finishes that should have been noticed by the buyer while the home was still on the dealers lot.

Many people apparently buy manufactured homes without closely inspecting them and are surprised to find later that the wall panels are fastened with staples that are still exposed on the surface, or they find there are no shelves under the bathroom vanities, or that the carpet is low grade, or there are lumps under the vinyl floor covers, etc.

And that brings up a very important point: If you notice a lot of loose wall trim, misaligned cabinet doors, lumps, cuts and/or patches in the vinyl floor covering, or torn or loose carpet that you can't live with, don't let the salesperson convince you that all those things will be repaired or replaced once the home is delivered to your home site. Many home manufacturers' warranties exclude some or all of the components or conditions described above, and the manufacturer will not correct them.

Unrepaired cuts and patches to vinyl floor covering

WARRANTIES

In many states every manufacturer must furnish the buyer with a warranty against significant defects in material and workmanship in their homes. Sometimes the law does not specify what constitutes a "significant defect" so many warranties cover only structural components. There are major differences in the warranties issued by the various manufacturers. Some manufacturers have good warranty coverage, good warranty service, and seldom have a complaint filed against them. Others have limited warranties and poor warranty service which results in numerous complaints to the state agencies and to HUD.

The Federal Magnuson-Moss Act requires a dealer to show you the warranty on any home prior to purchase. If the dealer or salesperson refuses to allow to see the warranty, run, don't walk, to your automobile and find yourself another dealer. You may wish to file a complaint with the Federal Trade Commission (FTC) by sending a letter to: Correspondence Branch, Federal Trade Commission, Washington, D.C. 20580 or by calling their nearest regional office. You can find a complete list of FTC regional offices at the back of this book in Appendix C.

— 3 —

WHAT TO LOOK FOR IN A USED HOME

What to look for in a used home can be summed up in one word: Everything. In addition to all of the topics discussed in Chapter 2 of this book, you should carefully examine Everything. In some states, including Arkansas, a dealer can sell a used home in any condition, from junkers to "completely rebuilt" homes. No agency inspects these homes for compliance to any code. Some dealers have taken burned out shells and thrown together what looked like mobile homes, and sold them without disclosing their history. In one particular case, the thrown-together piece of junk fell in on itself before it made to the buyer's home site. Another made it to a home site where the roof caved in a few weeks later.

Some states have very strict but reasonable standards for used homes sold off dealers' lots. Minimum standards for used homes sold in other states have been proposed but the industry has generally made sure no such regulations have been established.

After the flooding in the Mid-West and in the Southeast a few years ago, hundreds of flood damaged homes were purchased without titles and sold in Arkansas. The water damage was often concealed and the buyers were, in some cases, never told the origin or history of the home. The homes had no titles because insurance companies "totaled" the homes and took possession of the titles, and then gave the homes back to the original owners. The insurance companies didn't want the hassle and expense of moving them. The homes were sold dirt cheap by the original owners to get them off their property. The homes were resold by dealers at a substantial profit after new carpeting had been put down, some wainscot panels installed over the high water marks on the inside walls, and the high water marks on the outside scrubbed off. There are buyers still trying to get titles to these homes after they have paid them off.

The things you will need to look at in a used home are the same as those in a new one, except you must be aware there may be water or fire damage to floors, walls, and ceilings that have been covered with new paint, wall-board, ceiling board, trim, or carpet.

TIP The bottom line is: look *very* closely at everything and take your time doing it. In most states dealers are not required to give warranties on used homes. Some do, and honor their warranty. Many others show on the purchase agreement that the home, or part of it, is warranted but you will never get that warranty honored.

— 4 —

ABOUT THE
DELIVERY OF
YOUR HOME

If you have specially ordered a home from the factory, you should have a note put on the purchase agreement that you must inspect the home when it arrives on the dealer's lot. If the home has significant transportation damages or significant manufacturing defects, or if it does not have the special features or options that are shown on your purchase agreement, address the problems on the dealer's lot. The federal regulations require that any transportation damages and/or manufacturing defects to be corrected before the home is sold. It is easier for the service personnel to repair damages and correct defects while the home is still on the dealer's lot than trying to do that work at your home site.

If your purchase agreement includes options you paid for but which are not in the home, either accept the home without them and have the price of the options refunded to you or have them deleted from the retail installment contract. (That will mean a new contract will have to be drawn up by the lender.)

At the time you order a home, or agree to purchase one off the lot, you should insist that the dealer send someone familiar with delivering and installing homes to your site to see if the home can be put there. Make it clear to him that you know nothing about that and, since his people are the professionals, you want them to tell you if the delivery will cost you additional money for dozer or wrecker services.

Be sure there is access to the property that you have selected. If the dealer or his agent tells you that trees will have to be removed, a wider road built, or the site leveled, you will have to decide if that expense is worth having a mobile home put on the site.

The site should be well drained so that water does not run or stand under the home. **Never install a home on fill or loose dirt that has not been compacted**.

A home should not be placed under trees with limbs that will come in contact with the home at any place during high winds. Large overhanging

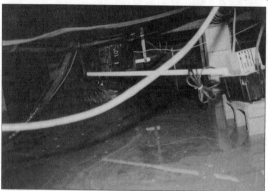

trees will cause premature deterioration of any type roof covering and will cause leaks if the tree leaves or needles accumulate on the roof. A metal roof will soon corrode and discolor from the tannic acid produced by the leaves of certain trees, especially oaks.

Eight feet of water standing under a new double-wide home. Note 10" heat duct floating in the water

Inspect the home very closely when it arrives on your property or lot. Look carefully at the roof and the vents and stacks attached to it. Have any of the seals been broken? Are the stacks standing straight? Is the roof smooth? Look at the outside walls and the underside of the home for transportation damages. If there is significant damage to the roof, walls, floor, or frame, do not allow the home to be installed until the dealer lot manager comes to the site to view the damages.

If there is serious damage to the home, you should not accept it. Do not make the mistake that others have made by accepting a home which has been severely damaged while being delivered to the home site, especially if you are being persuaded to accept it by the dealer or installer telling you all of the damage will be repaired by the factory under the home's warranty. That is a common tactic, a con job, and a cop out. Everyone familiar with the industry knows that the home's manufacturer *is not responsible for damage done to the home after it leaves the dealer's lot*.

If you have obtained financing for your home's purchase through a lending company which has a working relationship with the dealer, you should be very careful about when and how you notify the lender the home has been installed and that all the other goods and services you have financed through the loan have been delivered.

Usually most lenders will do what is known as a "phone audit" to confirm the fact that the home, goods, and services have *all* been delivered to the purchaser by the dealer. This usually occurs after the dealer has submitted the signed financing contract to the lending agency and asks the company to "fund" the deal (pay him for the home).

In some cases, dealers have asked that buyers complete the phone audit while the home is still sitting on the dealer's lot. Advice from the people who have been there and done that: *Never tell a lending agency that a home, goods, and services have been received if they have not.*

ABOUT INSTALLING
YOUR HOME

I have inspected more than one thousand homes which have been sold and installed in twelve states. Over 90% of those homes had significant defects and deficiencies in their installation.

Regulations in most states require a manufactured home to be installed in accordance with the home manufacturer's installation instruction. The federal regulations require the manufacturer's installation instructions for the support and anchoring systems be designed by a Registered Professional Engineer or Architect.

The federal regulations also require that the home buyer be given the installation instructions and the home owners manual at the time of sale. Some manufacturers combine the installation instructions and the home owners manual into one book. Those regulations also prohibit the dealer from interfering with the distribution of the manual(s), although many dealers and installers routinely withhold the installation instructions from the buyers to keep them from discovering the homes are not being properly installed.

The improper installation of any manufactured home can cause major damages to a home which will cost an arm and leg to correct. Improper installation of multi-sectional homes will result in major damages to the homes' structure. (I recently inspected a single-wide home that was defectively supported when it was installed two years earlier. The lack of adequate supports under the home caused the ceiling to split open across the full width of the home during the previous Christmas holidays. Of course that Christmas present was not well received by the home's owner.)

The sections of a double-wide home recently inspected in Alabama were found to be separating and moving in opposite directions because the foundations were settling abnormally; the roofs and the end-walls of the two halves were not structurally connected when installed.

Although each manufacturer's installation manual may be somewhat different, they all contain some of the same basic requirements. They may also contain descriptions of some installation methods and materials the manufacturer approves but which are not permitted by state regulations.

Unbelievably, some manufacturers' installation manuals allow the use of plywood for pier foundations. Most states' regulations require that pier foundations be solid concrete, either poured on site or pre-cast, with minimum dimensions of 4" X 16" X 16". Most homes are set on pre-cast "pad" blocks with the dimensions just specified. If possible, any mobile home that is installed on anything other than solid bedrock should be installed on poured concrete footings.

Many states now allow the use of ABS plastic pads for pier foundations. At present, not many dealers or installers use them because of their costs. They are designed to be used only under specified site conditions which are detailed in the pad manufacturer's installation instructions. In all of the installations I have inspected in which the ABS foundations were used, the soil at the site was not suitable for their use and the pads failed to properly support the homes. It remains to be seen if the misuse of these pads becomes a major problem nationwide, as I expect it will.

ABS plastic foundation pads
used on unsuitable soil

All properly prepared installation manuals specify and explain that the number and/or size of foundations that should be installed will depend on the load bearing capacity of the soil at the site. That's just common sense. Any intelligent builder knows that it will take more, or larger, foundations to support a structure in a swamp than to support a structure set on an outcrop of solid limestone in the Ozark mountains. In no case should a mobile home be set on loose dirt used as fill for a home site. Loose dirt has a minimal bearing capacity which will allow uneven settling of the foundations and cause the house to settle and become unlevel. The results are cracked ceilings, bowed floors and roof, and doors and windows that drag and bind. Leveling the home again without providing more piers or larger foundations is a waste of time and money.

Because there may be no one to do it for you, you should do the inspection of your home's installation yourself, preferably while the installation is being done. There is no "rocket science" involved in installing or inspecting the installation of a mobile home. Just about anyone can take the installation manual and read and understand the important parts.

There are a couple of basic things you need to know about the "Wind Zones" and "Roof Load Zones" that you will see mentioned in the manuals. The country is divided into three wind load zones and there are different construction and anchoring requirement for each zone. Most of the country is in WIND ZONE I, the other two wind zones cover coastal areas that are prone to hurricanes. The anchoring requirements for homes sited in Wind Zone I are significantly less stringent than the requirements for homes set in the other two zones.

There are three Roof Load (snow/ice) Zones which require different construction and support designs. You may see set-up instructions in the manufacturer's manual for all three zones because some of the larger manufacturers build and sell all over the country. Homes built for the South Roof Load Zone are designed to withstand only 20 pounds per square foot of snow loads (live load), plus the weight of the roof structure (dead load). See Appendix A at the back of this book, "Wind and Roof Load Zones by State."

INSTALLING A SINGLE-WIDE HOME

Inspecting the set-up and anchoring of a single-wide mobile home is relatively easy. Some of the most important things you should see in a properly installed mobile home are shown below. Always check the installation instructions to see if there are any unusual requirements for the set-up of the particular home purchased.

(a) Support piers under the I-beams should be spaced no more than eight feet (8') apart (or 10' apart if allowed by the instructions and state law permits it) and spaced much closer if the ground under the home is loose or soft.

(b) Each pier should have a concrete foundation that is at least 4" thick and 16" square. The foundations should be below the frost line for the area in which the home is installed. (Some states and local building codes require more elaborate foundation requirements.)

(c) The main portion of the pier should consist of concrete blocks which are nominally 8" X 8" x 16" in size. The blocks can be solid (seldom used) or open celled (normally used).

(d) The blocks do not have to have mortared joints, unless you have obtained a "permanent foundation" loan, or if local building codes require it. The dealer and/or lender should make that clear before the loan is approved.

(e) The instructions may allow the piers to be constructed with single blocks up to a height of three blocks. If a pier is more than three blocks high (not including solid pad or cap blocks), the instructions should specify how the piers are to be assembled. Usually "double-block" piers are required. (Two concrete blocks laid side-by-side in a layer, and the next two blocks laid in the same manner but crosswise to the previous layer.)

(f) When the total height of a pier (from the ground to the bottom of the I-beam) exceeds about 52 inches, the instructions will usually require the interlocking blocks to be filled with concrete and reinforced with 3/8" rebar metal.

(g) If any pier exceeds 80" in height, the instructions usually require the whole support system to be designed by a professional engineer or architect, and the plans submitted to the state or local building official having jurisdiction over the home's installation.

(h) A solid concrete cap block or wooden top plate is usually required on the top of each pier.

(i) 1" thick wooden shims and wooden wedges can be used on each pier to do the final level if the wedges are paired in reverse orientation (thin end on top of thick end) to produce a more even bearing surface for the bottom flange of the I-beam.

(j) No pier should be less than 12" in height, measured from the ground to the bottom of the I-beam.

(k) All piers should be plumb and level, and display acceptable workmanship in their construction. (No cracked or broken blocks, or pieces of scrap lumber, pieces of firewood, or rocks, etc.) (Don't laugh, its happened.)

(l) Piers are usually required directly under the jamb studs of each exterior door, including extra doors, such as french doors and patio doors.

I-beam support pier leaning.

Crossover heat duct on ground.

I-beam support leaning and about to fall

(m) There must be anchors installed under each side of the home and the straps connected to the I-beams. There is required to be an anchor within two feet (2') of each end of each I-beam and others spaced along the I-beam as specified in the manufacturer's installation manual. On single wide homes, the spacing varies, depending on how sturdy a frame and floor system the manufacturer chose to use. Some manufacturers require anchors at 8' spacings, other allow the anchors to be as much as 13' apart, depending on the wind zone in which the home is to be installed.

On multi-sectional homes placed in Wind Zone 1 anchors are very often required underneath the marriage line directly below the sides of the large openings through the mating walls inside the home. Anchors are always required at those locations if the home is sited in Wind Zones 2 or 3. For more on multi-sectional homes, *see* "Installing a Multi-Wide Home," below.

(n) The anchors must be the type approved for use in the soil (or rock) at the home site. The general requirements are that if an auger type anchor can be used, it should be used. Cross-drive (a set of two straight rods driven through a special, x-shaped head), are designed to be used only in rock, coral or consolidated (naturally cemented) gravel.

(o) If the home has factory installed, over-the-roof straps (straps that lie just under the exterior siding and with the loose ends usually coiled up under the edge of the sidewalls when the home arrives on site), they must also be connected to anchors in Wind Zone 2 or 3, and should be connected if the home is placed in Wind Zone 1.

Note: These over-the-roof straps are not to be used in lieu of frame anchor straps. Frame anchors must be installed as described in the installation manual. With properly installed anchoring and support systems, homes manufactured for Wind Zone 1 should be able to withstand winds of about 76 MPH. Homes properly designed, supported, and anchored for Wind Zone 2 and 3 should withstand 100 and 110 MPH winds respectively.

(p) Make sure the anchor straps are properly connected to the frame and the straps are tensioned.

Anchor strap connector fell off I-beam because it was not properly wrapped and connected

There are several types of anchor strap-to-frame connecting devices. The most common is a "j" shaped hook (or "clamp") that is to be hooked to the outside, bottom flange of the I-beam and the strap should run upward behind the I-beam and then over the top of the beam to the anchor head. *This type of buckle should not be connected to the inside, bottom flange of the I-beam and then run directly to the anchor head. If the home settles, the stiffness of the strap will force the hook off the I-beam flange.*

Another connecting device is a clamp with double jaws that fits around the bottom flange of the I-beam and the strap should run directly to the anchor head.

Still another device is one that resembles a belt buckle. The anchor strap is run through the two slots in the buckle, over the I-beam, back through the buckle, the strap then pulled tight so the buckle is close to the I-beam, and the loose end run to the anchor head.

In no case should the anchor strap be connected to the I-beam as one jack-leg installer in northeast Arkansas was prone to do. That "installer" bent the ends of the straps into a hook and draped the bent ends of the straps over the tops of the I-beams. Needless to say, the strap was not capable of resisting the allowable, minimum working load of 3,150 pounds required by the HUD Code and state regulations. In fact, the straps could not be effectively used as a leash for a poodle.

If a part of a home's frame is installed unusually high off the ground, special anchor installation instructions in the manual must be followed.

A Note on Using Installation Manuals: Most installation manuals outline step-by-step procedures for the home's installation but the instructions are sometimes over-simplified and sometimes omit important details or steps. Some of these manuals even omit steps that are required by the HUD Code.

INSTALLING A MULTI-WIDE HOME

The proper installation of a multi-wide home is not a simple task and it requires a great deal of expertise. Experience sometimes leads installers to believe they don't need to look at the installation instructions. That attitude usually means a home is installed the way the installer thinks it should be, rather than being installed the way an engineer or architect has designed it to be put together, blocked and anchored. Some of the better installers are young people who have read the manuals and understand the reasons for doing what is required by the manuals.

The requirements for I-beam support, blocking under exterior doors, and anchoring for multi-sectional homes are basically the same as for single-wide home, except that instead of two I-beams to support, there will be four (in a double-wide) or six (in a triple-wide). One other difference is that the required spacing of frame anchors is not as close for multi-section homes as for single-wide homes. (Multi-section homes are less likely to be displaced by wind because of their overall width relative to their length.)

The critical differences in the support of multi-sectional homes are the requirements to place pier supports under the mating line of the floors, directly under each side of wall opening through the mating line. Generally, all openings through the marriage walls that are four feet (4') or more in width must have what are called "ridge beam column support piers" installed under the edges of the opening. The piers are needed at those locations because there are multiple wall studs beside each opening that are glued and fastened together and which support a ridge beam in the ceiling above the opening. Each group of multiple studs are called "column supports or posts." Each half of the home usually has its own ridge beam, which matches the one on the opposite side. The vertical "king post" on the ends of the roof trusses above the marriage wall openings are fastened to the ridge beams. That means the weight of the roof/ceiling system above the openings on each half of the home is being transferred to the ridge beams. The ridge beams in turn transfer that load to the tops of the column support columns, which in turn transfers the load to the floor. If no piers are placed directly under the column supports, the concentrated load of the roof/ceiling on the columns will only be transferred to the floor and not to the ground. The loads will cause the floors of the two halves to sag at those locations. The lack of support under the column posts will also cause the roof and ceiling to sag and will eventually break the ceiling board and cause damage to the roof trusses.

Marriage wall of a double-wide section

Ridge beam support columns.
Front ½   Back ½
Marriage line

**Ridge beam support column
on one side of clear span opening
through marriage wall**

Marriage line pier under ridge beam column

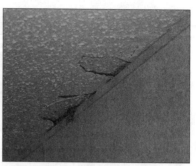

Ceiling board damaged due to lack of support under ridge beam columns

Manufacturers usually require that the marriage line also be supported within a couple of feet of the ends of the homes.

Some of the other most important requirements for installing multi-sectional home are as follows:

> (a) *Before the sections are put together some method must be used to seal the mating line joints between the floors, both end walls, and the ceilings of the sections.*

The requirement for sealing the joints in the living space envelope of multi-sectional homes when they are joined together comes directly from the HUD Code. If the requirement is not spelled out in the manufacturer's installation manual, the manual itself is defective and in error. (And many manuals are defective in that regard.)

It is very important that the mating surfaces of the ceiling line, the floor line and the mating line between the walls be sealed to prevent air and moisture infiltration into the home and to prevent the loss of conditioned (heated or cooled) air from the living space.

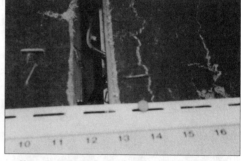

Unsealed marriage line joint between end walls of a double-wide

Many installers never seal the ceiling line joints before the home is put together and it is virtually impossible to properly seal the ceiling joints later. Please note that installing interior trim over the ceiling's mating line joint at marriage wall openings inside the home is not the same thing as sealing the ceiling's mating line joint. The rest of the ceiling's mating line joint is concealed behind the tops of the marriage walls. The joint must be sealed before the sections are joined and connected.

During an inspection of a home involved in a consumer complaint in north Arkansas, I overheard the home's installer tell another inspector who was with me, "I don't bother to seal the ceiling line joint because I seal the joint between the peak of the two roof sections with batt, fiberglass insulation." It had never dawned on the installer that inserting fiberglass insulation at the roof peak mating joint was totally a waste of time and materials because the attic cavity was ventilated. (All shingled roof cavities must be ventilated per the HUD Code.) The outside air that ventilated the attic was also infiltrating the interior marriage wall cavity through the unsealed marriage line joint between the ceilings of the two sections.

The installation manual may show more than one acceptable method (or material) for sealing these joints. The failure to seal the mating joints will result in excessive utility bills and will result in major damage to the marriage wall framing and to the interior wallboard from moisture condensation inside the marriage wall cavities.

When the floor, ceiling, or endwall mating lines are not sealed, moisture accumulates in the stud bays of the marriage walls and condenses inside the wall cavity during the summer. In the winter, the moisture in the air inside the home condenses on the interior surface of the marriage wall. In most cases, the moisture accumulation will cause the marriage wall studs, the bottom plates, the wallboard and the floor to bow, mildew, and eventually rot.

When the floor's mating line is not sealed under the openings through the marriage line, moisture will condense on the underside of the carpet and carpet pad, causing the carpet to mildew and rot.

(b) *The floors of the sections must be securely fastened along the mating line.*

The installation manual will show one or more acceptable methods of connecting the floors of the two halves. Commonly, 3/8" or 5/16" lag screws are installed through the floor system's marriage line perimeter joists (commonly called "rim" joists) of the section into the perimeter joist of the other section. If this is the method the manufacturer chooses to put in his manual, the manufacturer must supply the lag screws. The installation manual will usually specify the screws be spaced no more that two feet apart (sometimes closer) and that the screws be staggered. (One driven through from one rim joist, the next driven through from the opposite joist.)

Sometimes the manufacturer may weld connector plates to the mating sides of the frame so that bolts and nuts can be used to connect the halves together at the floors' mating line. In most cases, these plates will not align and are useless for the purpose intended.

(c) *The roof peaks of the sections must be fastened as specified in the installation instructions.*

The instructions usually require the roof sections be connected at the peak by lag screws of a specified diameter and length, spaced at specific intervals, and usually staggered from one side to the other. The screws penetrate either the ridge beams or other roof framework. (Some manufacturers use continuous ridge beams on both halves. Most don't.)

Some manufacturer's allow the sections to be connected at the roof-mating line by attaching galvanized metal straps across the mating joint. The straps are to be of a specified minimum thickness (usually 31 gage) and fastened as described in the instructions. (Several double-wide homes inspected in Alabama during the Summer of 2001 were found to "structurally connected" at the roof mating line by aluminum foil which had been stapled over the mating line joint. Of course, the method was designed by the installer, not by the home's manufacturer.)

Roof sections of a double-wide only connected by aluminum foil fastened with roof tacks

Sections of a double-wide home not structurally connected at roof peak

(d) *Most manufacturers require the mating, endwall studs on each end of the home to be securely connected. The fastening methods vary and the instructions in the installation manual should be followed.*

(e) *In a few manuals, the mating studs beside the openings through the marriage line are required to be fastened also. In most manuals, fastening at these points is not required.*

(f) *The cross-over electrical wiring connections between the sections of a home should be made in electrical junction boxes with covers if wire nuts connections are used. If special connectors are used, such as "Amp™" brand connectors, the connections do not have to be made inside junction boxes, but in no case should the crossover wiring or the connections be exposed under the home. The HUD Code, the National Electric Code, and the manufacturer's installation instructions require electrical cables not be exposed under the home. If the cables and connections are not concealed in the sub-floor cavity, the wiring must be protected with rigid metal conduit. (About 95% of all the multi-sectional homes I have inspected on site were found to have electrical wiring dangling below the floor's mating line.)*

Crossover electrical cables left exposed and dangling below a floors' mating line. (Many of the connectors are defectively installed also.)

(g) *The crossover heat duct must be kept off the ground. It is a HUD Code requirement which must be addressed in all manufacturer's installation instructions. If the plastic covered and insulated crossover duct is not supported off the ground it will deteriorate prematurely, and moisture will condense inside the duct during cold weather.*

(h) *The bare, grounding conductor that is required by the HUD Code should be clamped to the frame of one section when the multi-sectional home leaves the factory and must be clamped to the frame of the other section(s) when the home is installed. The grounding (or bonding) conductor prevents the frames of the sections from becoming energized if a short circuit to the frame occurs.*

It should be noted that the HUD Code requires that the electrical grounding system be isolated from the neutral side of the electrical supply system (sheathing on the neutral conductors should be white) inside a manufactured home. Unlike the electrical systems in other types of homes and buildings, the grounding and neutral conductors should only be connected at the electrical service entrance outside the home. (The service entrance is often called the "meter loop.") It requires a four-wire wiring system from the home to the meter to properly connect the home to power. The installation instructions should fully explain how the connections between the home and electrical supply are to be made.

(i)   *If the manufactured has not connected all of the sub-floor DWV (drain-waste-vent) lines to bring them to one 3" drop-out, all of the fittings, strapping, solvent cements, piping, and the drawings and instructions to assemble and connect them is required to be furnished with the home. Some state regulations require the installer to assemble and support the piping to bring it to one 3" drop-out as specified in the instructions. It is part of the home's installation, but many dealer's and installer refuse to connect and assemble the DWV lines to bring them to a single 3" drop-out.*

Many dealer's have home buyers sign an agreement that assigns the buyers the responsibility for finishing that part of the home's installation. The agreement usually includes a statement by the dealer that state law does not allow the dealership to connect the plumbing because the dealer's employees are not licensed plumbers. The statement is generally not true. Many dealers in Alabama and Arkansas and other southern states use this ruse so that they do not have to connect the DWV system. It is particularly ironic when used in Alabama. The HUD Code specifies that the DWV system is part of the home and its installation until it is terminated at a single 3" drop. The HUD Code preempts the states from establishing any more stringent standards for a manufactured home's DWV system. It would be ludicrous for the state of Alabama to require that a licensed plumber connect the "ship-

Unsupported DWV piping

loose" portion of the DWV when the rest of the plumbing in the homes built in the numerous plants in Alabama is installed by persons having no license or certification from the state to do such work. (The Manufactured Housing Commissions in most states have oversight authority regarding the installation of the DWV piping that is part of a manufactured home.)

If, as sometimes happens, a dealer or installer keeps the plumbing piping, fittings and supplies which were shipped with the home and tries to sell them back to you, talk to your Prosecuting Attorney; that's theft of your property!

> (j) *If the dealer has included the price of skirting and its installation in the price of the home, be sure to read the Home Owner's Manual and/or the Manufacturer's Installation Manual to see what steps must be taken to control moisture in the crawl space when skirting is installed.*

Most manuals contain specific conditions which *must be met* when a home is skirted. Most manuals specify that *the home's warranty will be voided* if the required conditions are not met.

Generally, manufacturers' instructions require the following described conditions be met when a home is skirted. Check the manuals for variations that might be included.

> (i) A vapor barrier ground cover must be installed on the entire surface of the ground under the home. The vapor barrier specified is usually polyethylene sheeting (roll plastic, clear or black) or asphalt roofing underlayment ("tar" paper). The manuals usually require any seams in the vapor barrier be over-lapped at least 6". If it is known at the time the home is being installed that it is to be skirted, the vapor barrier is usually required to be put down before the pad block foundations are installed.

> (ii) There must be vents installed in the skirting with the total free vent area to be equal to or exceed one square foot for every 150 square feet of floor area. Some manufacturer's manuals fail to specify the net free area needed for venting, although 1 sq. ft. per 150 sq. ft. of floor space is recommended.

(iii) If there is a clothes dryer in the home, the exhaust must terminate outside the skirting.

(iv) If an air conditioner is installed, and the "A" coil is installed in the furnace compartment, make absolutely sure the drain line from the "A" coil's condensation pan terminates outside the home, not in the crawl space, i.e., outside the skirting.

   The failure to control moisture in the crawl space is the major source of floor decking damage and deterioration (especially particle board) in mobile homes. Excessive sweating on windows and doors in the winter are indications you need to do more to control the moisture in the crawl space.

(k) *If your home has a factory installed fireplace the above-roof sections of the chimney are usually "shipped loose" inside the home and are attached on site as part of the home's installation. There is a storm collar which must be installed around the outer wall of the chimney just above the metal flashing through which the chimney passes. The home's installers must seal the joint between the storm collar and the outer wall of the flue pipe or there will be rainwater leakage into the concealed space inside the fireplace compartment. Usually the leakage around the unsealed storm collars cause major damage to the*

Storm collar lifted to show path of rainwater leakage into fireplace compartment

floors and walls of a home before the leakage is detected. If the leakage contacts the fireplace fan's electrical connections, a serious safety hazard can result.

— 6 —

SPECIAL INSTALLATION CONSIDERATIONS

This chapter is small but contains some very important information, if it applies to the particular home you purchased.

The first subject in this chapter is *"racking" or "racked,"* as applied to a section, or sections, of a multi-section mobile home. The dictionary meaning of the word rack is: *"To become forced out of shape or out of plumb."* But, in the mobile home industry, the word is often used to mean exactly the opposite of the dictionary meaning.

Now before the reader gets on his or her high-horse and says, "Who gives a d***?," bear with me a minute; it could help you understand why an installer is popping the siding and wallboard off your new multi-section home while trying to get the sections to fit together.

The bare frame for a mobile home is designed and built to have contours in it so that when the expected finished weight of the home is put on it, the frame becomes nearly straight. The contours built into the frame are called its *camber*. The frame usually has some camber left, especially at the tail-light end of the home or section, when the home is completed.

The camber is put in the main I-beams by running heavy, welding beads across the exposed surface of the top flanges. The amount of camber needed to keep the frame from "drooping" in transit depends on the expected weight of the home or section. Putting the camber in the frame is not an exact science and many times there is either too much or too little. Most often, its too much. When that happens, the tail-light end of the frame and the structure of the home itself curls upward like a stinging scorpion's tail.

Sometimes the camber in the tail-light end of one section of a multi-sectional home is very different than the camber in the other section(s). When an installer tries to bring the two sections together, they won't fit. At that point, the installer will usually jack up one end of one or both of the I-beams under one half to force that section to fit the other. That is what is usually called "racking" by dealers and installers.

They sometimes use the term "racked" to describe the condition of a home section that has walls that are not plumb in relation to the floor. That may also be due to the amount of camber in the frame. Some manufacturing plants level the frame and floor system by pulling the ends of the frame down with winches or hydraulic devices connected to anchoring points imbedded in the concrete floor of the plant. If this is not done when the exterior siding is being installed on a home with excess camber, the fastening of the sheathing to the wall studs will lock the camber in place and the home cannot be leveled, or fitted to the mating sections.

In some cases, unusual transportation stresses will cause the frame of a home or section to flex and bend. If it happens to a section, its not going to fit the other section when it gets on site.

The point of all this is: *Sometimes sections of multi-sectional homes cannot be closely fitted together by normal installation methods. "Racking" a badly misaligned section of a home to force it to fit a section that has a level floor and walls that are plumb can, and probably will, result in structural damage, some of which may not be apparent at the time.* (Stressed roof or wall framing may later fail with a loud "pop" in the middle of the night, any there may be split ceiling board or wall paneling to show for it the next morning.)

A little background information will help you understand the reasons for the special blocking requirements discussed below.

The HUD Code does not prescribe how the floor and frame of a manufactured home must be designed and built. The HUD Code only requires the roof, ceilings, floors and walls withstand certain wind loads (straight winds and uplift), snow, expected occupancy loads, etc. The manufacturer is responsible for obtaining approved engineering calculations and designs, and/or approved test data, to show the home will withstand the specified loads *when the home is supported and anchored in the field.*

The result of there being no prescriptive standards, but simply performance standards, is there are as many different frames and floor systems as there are blackbirds in a rice field after harvest. Some mobile home manufacturers choose to build homes on relatively weak frame/floor systems that will only withstand the loads specified in the HUD Code if the perimeter of the home is supported at the same intervals as the I-beams. (Perimeter piers are installed just under the sidewalls and in contact with the bottom edge of the perimeter joist.)

The manufacturers who build homes with frames and floor systems that must be perimeter blocked do so simply to save a few dollars. Most manufacturers stopped building frames and floors that required the extra blocking several years ago, but there are still homes sold that require perimeter blocking.

If these homes are not perimeter blocked, the floor system will "crown" over the center of the home or section as the unsupported weight of the roof loads on the sidewalls causes the floor system to sag along both sides. That condition is very costly to remedy if it is not addressed quickly.

If a particular brand, or model, of a home requires perimeter blocking, that information must be given to home buyers. It is usually specified in the installation manual, although not always clearly. The installation manuals for homes from some plants contain a statement which basically states that if a particular home requires perimeter blocking, the serial number of the home will contain the letter "P." (I'll tell you where to find the serial number a little later.)

Some manufacturers place a special label on the outside of the home near the HUD label to alert you or the installer to the fact the home requires perimeter blocking.

Other manufacturers write or type a note on the margins of the Data Plate (or Compliance Certificate) if their homes, or certain models, must be perimeter blocked.

In the worst case scenario, the manufacturer's installation instructions will contain an obscure remark that says if the home has I-beams that are spaced a certain distance apart, the home must be perimeter blocked.

Check closely to see if the home you are thinking of buying requires perimeter blocking. **If it does, make absolutely certain the home is installed in accordance with the installation manual**.

Some other special blocking requirements:

(a) If you know you are going to have very heavy furniture or a heavy water bed in a particular room; ask the installers to place extra piers under the I-beams and perimeter joists in that area. Rock and mortar fireplaces also need to have additional support blocking. (Many manuals specify additional blocking under such items.)

(b) If your home has a porch or a recessed entry door, special supports at those locations are nearly always required by the installation instructions.

7

OBTAINING WARRANTY SERVICE

As previously mentioned, each home manufacturer issues some type of a warranty for the homes produced. A warranty is not required by the HUD Code or by the Manufactured Home Procedural and Enforcement Regulations. The primary reason that a warranty is issued is the fact that FHA and VA financing agreements require the manufacturer to warranty the home for at least one year and ten days. Most warranties provide coverage for "substantial defects in materials and workmanship." Some manufacturers' warranties exclude carpet, vinyl floor coverings, trim, and other nonstructural components. Also generally excluded are appliances of all kind, such as ranges, furnaces, refrigerators, water heaters, range hoods, bath vent fans, etc. Those appliances are usually covered by the appliance manufacturers' warranties which the home's manufacturer is required to give to the buyer.

One thing should be pointed out here. If any of the above appliances fail to operate, or operate improperly, because they were not properly installed, or because they were damaged when installed at the manufactured home plant, the home manufacturer is responsible for their repair or replacement, not the appliance manufacturer.

You should read the home owner's manual and warranty before you buy a home and again immediately after you move into the home. If neither of those documents tell you who to contact for warranty service, you should look of the Data Plate (or Compliance Certificate) which is permanently attached to some wall or cabinet door inside the home. It is usually an 8-1/2" X 11", printed form which shows the manufacturer's name and address (sometimes a telephone number for warranty service), the home's model number, the HUD label number(s), the home's serial number, the date the home was completed, and other technical information. You should be able to get the telephone number for the factory's warranty service department from the dealer if it is not available in the home.

When you find defects in the home that you believe are covered by the warranty you should call or write the service manager at the plant that built the home. Carefully explain what the problems are and their location. (Keep a written record of warranty service requests made by phone, including a brief description of the problem, when the request was made, and the name and title of the person to whom the request was made.) If the problem is a **potential safety hazard** to the occupants, you should call the dealer's service manager immediately to report it. Explain the problem and ask him or her to have a service person sent as soon as possible to correct the problem. If the service manager does not let you know within a few hours as to when a service person can be there, call the lot manager. If you get no real response from him quickly, call the service manager at the plant that produced the home. Safety hazards must be addressed in a timely manner by the manufacturer. If the manufacturer fails to investigate and make the necessary repairs or corrections to eliminate an imminent safety hazard in a reasonable time, the home owners may, under the provisions of the Federal Regulations, hire a qualified person or firm to make the necessary repairs, and require the manufacturer to reimburse them for the expense. If a manufacturer refuses to reimburse the home owners for the expense under those conditions, the matter should be made the subject of a formal complaint to your State Administrative Agency (SAA) (see Appendix B.2 at the back of this book for a list of SAA's) or, if your state has no such agency, make the formal complaint to HUD at the address shown in Appendix B.1.

Some manufacturer's have agreements with their dealers which obligate the dealer's service department to perform the factory warranty service. In most cases the dealers are given a discount off the price of the home for doing the warranty service. Many of the larger dealerships with multiple lots have such agreements. If the dealer is responsible for doing the factory's warranty work, the buyer should be told that up front.

Having a local dealer's service department making the warranty repairs on your home can be a benefit to you if the service staff know what they are doing and do the work properly. If the dealer's service people are botching the service work or creating more problems than they are solving, the dealer should be notified. If the dealer fails to adequately address your concerns, and more service work is rendered in the same manner, begin putting your warranty service requests in writing and send them directly to the Service Manager at the plant that built your home. It is not necessary for you to send a copy of the correspondence to the dealer. The manufacturer is responsible for the warranty service on your home. If the manufacturer wants to take the matter up with the dealer, let him do so. You simply request that your warranty service work be done by the manufacturer's service people who should know how to properly correct defects in the home.

The most common complaints about the warranty service on mobile homes are shown below, along with a few suggestions as to how to handle certain warranty service situations if you are unfortunate enough to get involved in them.

(a) *Warranty service appointments are not kept, even when the home owners make it clear they are losing wages to be at home for the appointments.*

The first time you call for warranty service, ask that a note be placed in your file that makes it clear you will have to miss work to be at home and the service persons will need to keep their appointments. Also make it known how much advance notice you will require to make arrangements to be away from your job. You should be as reasonable as possible in setting these conditions as it is very difficult for the service people to adhere to rigid schedules. They never know what will be involved in a service call scheduled the day before yours. It is not always possible for them to leave an uncompleted job to meet the next appointment.

If the service people repeatedly fail to make their scheduled appointments, call the Service Manager and complain. If that does not help, call the plant's General Manager.

If it continues to happen, you may wish to file a claim in the Small Claims Court in your county against the manufacturer for your lost wages.

(b) *Warranty service work is done in a slip-shod or high-handed manner.*

I could devote an entire book to the stories relayed to me by home owners who were reportedly forced to contend with arrogant, abusive, and incompetent factory warranty service managers and service people. Several chapters of

such a book could be devoted to the same kind of stories which were documented and verified by me in following up behind such service people while I myself did factory warranty service repairs over a ten state area for about one year. Dealing with such warranty service personnel can be frustrating beyond belief and can try the patience of a saint. (To imply that I personally have the patience of a saint in dealing with such people would likely cause some service managers I've dealt with in an official capacity to collapse in fits of convulsive rage or maniacal laughter.)

The only advice I can offer to a home owner is to complain in writing to the manufacturer's service manager if you are mistreated in any way by a service person or if that person's work displays a lack of skills or workmanship. If that doesn't help, call the plant's General Manager. If that doesn't solve the problem, call the manu-

Factory warranty "service men" attempted to "adjust" front door frame so door would latch

facturer's corporate office and speak to the corporate official in charge of warranty services or customer complaints.

There have been times when home owners have rightfully ordered factory service personnel out of their home. No home owner is obligated to sit and watch an incompetent service person damage their home or personal property, or take verbal abuse from them. Some factory warranty service personnel have master keys to the homes built by the manufacturer and use them to enter home's without the owners' knowledge or consent when no one is at home. Those actions have not been well received by some owners who have

Factory warranty "service men" attempted to stop leak at windows. Leak not stopped!

called the police and had the service person explain why he or she should not be charged with burglary.

I should mention that I know many people who do factory warranty service work. Some of them are professionals who do excellent work and are highly respected by home owners and by people in and out of the industry. As unbelievable as some of the stories are that reflect negatively on the profession, there are some true stories about the extraordinary care and compassion some service people have shown, especially to the elderly, in performing their duties. Those people have my utmost respect and admiration. I hope anyone who buys a new home is fortunate enough to have some of those people perform their warranty service work.

(c) *Months after warranty service work has been requested, the manufacturer will not send service people to repair the home.*

Quit wasting your time and money on telephone calls and file a complaint with your state's SAA or your state's consumer protection agency. The agencies may do no more than what you have already done (they may simply notify the dealer and manufacturer of the complaint and file your complaint), but at least your complaints are now public record. That may help you later if the complaints are not resolved and you are forced to seek legal assistance.

(d) *The manufacturer has refused to correct significant manufacturing defects even after having been directed to do so by your state's SAA.*

Flexible flashing for toilet vent damaged at the factory, allowed rainwater leakage

If the Agency has directed the manufacturer to correct specific construction defects, and the time given the manufacturer to do so has elapsed, send written notification to the Agency Director of the situation. Specifically advise the Director if the work that was required to be done has not been satisfactorily completed and that you wish to have the home inspected (or re-inspected) by the agency's inspectors.

Some states have a Manufactured Housing Recovery Fund which can be used to repair your home if the manufacturer is unable or unwilling to make warranty repairs. In those states, when the warranty services cannot be obtained, an owner should file a claim against the manufacturer's Recovery Fund deposit. If the Agency refuses to file the claim on your behalf, seek legal assistance in pursuing your claim against the Recovery Fund and ask that the attorney file a complaint against the Agency's Director for refusing to process your claim.

If you do not have the resources to obtain legal assistance, and you believe the manufacturer and the SAA are not fulfiling their obligations in addressing your problems you should call or write:

> Manufactured Housing & Standards Division
> Office of Consumer & Regulatory Affairs
> Department of Housing and Urban Development
> 451 Seventh Street, S.W., Mail Room B133
> Washington, D. C. 20410
> Telephone (202) 708-6409 or (202) 755-7430
> Fax   (202) 708-4213

8

MAINTAINING AND CARING FOR YOUR HOME

A mobile home buyer should make sure they receive the home owner's manual and read it carefully. Most manuals specify that the home's warranty will be voided if the home owner fails to follow some of the use and maintenance instructions that are included in it. Typically the owner is responsible for insuring that the conditions or actions described below are met or taken:

1. The site around the home is sloped or otherwise altered to prevent rainwater from running under the home.
2. Trees or limbs should not be in contact with the home, and leaves should not be allowed to accumulate on the roof.
3. The clothes dryer exhaust must terminate outside the home.
4. Kerosene heaters should not be used inside the home.
5. The furnace and/or air conditioner filter should be kept clean.
6. The seams, joints, and edges of metal roofs must be inspected and sealed as specified in the manual.
7. Hardboard or other types of wood siding should be sealed and/or painted as specified in the manual.
8. Use the bathroom ventilation fans when bathing.

9. Do not keep an unusually large number of plants in the home.

10. Make sure the crawl space under the home is adequately ventilated.

11. See that the "whole house ventilation" feature is used as described in the home owner's manual.

Owners should pay particular attention to the type of "whole house ventilation" systems that may be installed. There are some mechanical systems that provide fresh air to the interior of the home and ventilate the roof cavity (attic) at the same time. The systems depends on roof-mounted fan assemblies to circulate fresh air from outside through the attic and into the home. The fans are controlled by timers which cycle the fans' operations on and off at four hour intervals, or they are controlled by thermostats and humidistats inside the assembly. The units sometimes have switches in the furnace compartments that turn them off, put them in the automatic mode or allow the unit to be controlled manually. When those types of devices are used for attic ventilation, there are usually only small ventilation openings into the attic at the ends of the home. If those units fail to operate properly, there will be inadequate ventilation of the attic, and there will be major damage to the roof/ceiling systems due to excessive accumulations of heat and moisture inside the attic.

Air intake screen on attic ventilator blocked with dust and debris

I have inspected numerous homes which utilize the mechanical system, rather than a row of static vents along the peak of the roof and ventilation openings in the sidewall eave soffits. Many of the homes were experiencing roof/ceiling problems because the attic ventilation systems were defectively installed, damaged or the ventilation openings blocked off. In most cases the blockage of the ventilation openings cannot be seen from the ground.

Because of the problems often associated with these types of "whole house and attic ventilation" systems, I do not recommend them as the sole source for attic ventilation. If they are used on the home you purchase, you should check to see that:

One of the attic ventilation openings blocked with dust and debris

- There are actually openings into the attic cavity at the ends of the home. There may be vents at the ends of the roof or ventilation openings in the rake eave soffits (the soffits under the roof overhang at the ends of the home). *If the openings are in the soffits, loosen the soffit material to see that there are also openings into the attic cavity from the roof overhang cavity.*

- The fan in the unit actually works, and that the controls shut the fan off at regular intervals, or when the attic is cool at night.
- The air intake screens underneath the metal caps of the roof-mounted fan assembly are not blocked with dust and debris.

Gold metal cover under eave shows continuous strip soffit vent

During a recent series of home inspections in the states of Alabama and Georgia, I found one attic ventilator fan that had never been connected to power, one that would not operate because it had been damaged at the mobile home plant, and one whose screened opening was completely blocked by dust and air-borne debris. In several homes the home manufacturer failed to provide unobstructed ventilated openings into the attic cavity.

There may be other maintenance and use requirements in the owners manual that are critical to the durability of the home.

Manufactured home warranties do not cover damages resulting from abuse or neglect of the home, or damages done to the home while it is being moved from the original home site. Many warranties are voided if the home is moved to another location during the warranty period.

Appendix A

WIND AND ROOF LOAD ZONES BY STATE

A.1 WIND ZONES BY STATE

Wind Zone III ... 110 mph. The following areas are considered to be within Wind Zone III of the Basic Wind Zone Map:

> States and Territories: The entire **State of Hawaii**, the **coastal regions of Alaska** (as determined by the 90 mph isotach on the ANSI/ASCE 7-88 map), and all of the U.S. Territories of **American Samoa**, **Guam**, **Northern Mariana Islands**, **Puerto Rico**, **Trust Territory of the Pacific Islands**, and the **United States Virgin Islands**.

Local governments: The following local governments listed by State (counties, unless specified otherwise):

> **Florida**: Broward, Charlotte, Collier, Dade, Franklin, Gulf, Hendry, Lee, Martin, Manatee, Monroe, Palm Beach, Pinellas, and Sarasota.

> **Louisiana**: Parishes of Jefferson, Lafourche, Orleans, Plaquemines, St. Bernard, St. Charles, St. Mary, and Terrabonne.

> **North Carolina**: Carteret, Dare, and Hyde.

Wind Zone II ...100 mph. *The following areas are deemed to be within Wind Zone II of the Basic Wind Zone Map:*

Local governments: The following local governments listed by State (counties, unless specified otherwise):

Alabama: Baldwin and Mobile.

Florida: All counties except those identified as within Wind Zone III.

Georgia: Bryan, Camden, Chatham, Glynn, Liberty, McIntosh.

Louisiana: Parishes of Acadia, Allen, Ascension, Assumption, Calcasieu, Cameron, East Baton Rouge, East Feliciana, Evangeline, Iberia, Iberville, Jefferson Davis, Lafayette, Livingston, Pointe Coupee, St. Helena, St. James, St. John the Baptist, St. Landry, St. Martin, St. Tammany, Tangipahoa, Vermilion, Washington, West Baton Rouge, and West Feliciana.

Maine: Hancock and Washington.

Massachusetts: Barnstable, Bristol, Dukes, Nantucket, and Plymouth.

Mississippi: George, Hancock, Harrison, Jackson, Pearl River, and Stone.

North Carolina: Beaufort, Brunswick, Camden, Chowan, Columbus, Craven, Currituck, Jones, New Hanover, Onslow, Pamlico, Pasquotank, Pender, Perquimans, Tyrrell, and Washington.

South Carolina: Beaufort, Berkeley, Charleston, Colleton, Dorchester, Georgetown, Horry, Jasper, and Williamsburg.

Texas: Aransas, Brazoria, Calhoun, Cameron, Chambers, Galveston, Jefferson, Kenedy, Kleberg, Matagorda, Nueces, Orange, Refugio, San Patricio, and Willacy.

Virginia: Cities of Chesapeake, Norfolk, Portsmouth, Princess Anne, and Virginia Beach.

Wind Zone I. Wind Zone I consists of those areas on the Basic Wind Zone Map that are not identified as being within Wind Zone II or III, respectively.

A.2 SNOW LOAD ZONES BY STATE

North (40 pounds per square feet):

Alaska

Maine: Northern two-thirds of the state.

Middle (30 pounds per square feet):

Colorado

Idaho

Iowa: Northern third, except for northeast corner of the state.

Maine: Southern third of the state.

Massachusetts: Northern-most tip of the state.

Michigan: Northern quarter of the state and the upper peninsula.

Minnesota: All, except northwest corner and southeast corner of the state which are classified as South.

Montana

New Hampshire

New York: Northern half of the state.

South Dakota: Eastern quarter except for northeast corner of the state.

Utah

Vermont: All but a small southern portion of the state.

Wisconsin: Northern half of the state.

Wyoming

South (20 pounds per square feet):

The rest of the United States.

Appendix B

HUD AND STATE ADMINISTRATIVE AGENCIES (SAAs) INFORMATION

B.1 HUD INFORMATION

Manufactured Housing & Standards Division
Office of Consumer and Regulatory Affairs
US Department of Housing and Urban Development
451 Seventh Street, SW
Rm. 9152
Washington, DC 20410-8000
Telephone: (202) 708-6423 or 1-800-927-2891.
FAX: (202) 708-4213
Email: MHS@hud.gov

B.2 STATE ADMINISTRATIVE AGENCIES (SAAs) INFORMATION

ALABAMA
Mr. Jim Sloan, Administrator
Alabama Manufactured Housing Commission
350 S. Decatur Street
Montgomery, AL 36104-4306
PH: 334-242-4036 ext 22 or 25
FAX: 334-240-3178 Email:
jsloan@amhc.state.al.us

ALASKA — Use HUD address above.

ARIZONA
Mr. N. Eric Borg, Director
Department of Building & Fire Safety
Office of Manufactured Housing
99 East Virginia, Suite #100
Phoenix, AZ 85004-1108
PH: 602-255-4072, ext. 244
FAX: 602-255-4962
Email: azdbfs@netzone.com

ARKANSAS
Mr. Whit Waller, Director
Arkansas Manufactured Home Commission
523 South Louisiana Street, Suite 500
Little Rock, AR 72201-5705
PH: 501-324-9032
FAX: 501-324-9034

CALIFORNIA
Mr. Richard Weinert, Administrator
    Street Address:
Dept of Housing & Community Development
1800 Third Street, Suite 260
Manufactured Housing Section Sacramento,
CA 95814-6900
P.O. Box 31
Sacramento, CA 95812-0031
PH: 916-445-3338 (DD) 916-327-2838
FAX: 916-327-4712
Email: rweinert@hcd.ca.gov

COLORADO
Mr. Tom Hart, Director
Housing Division, Dept of Local Affairs
1313 Sherman Street, #518
Denver, CO 80203-2244
PH: 303-866-2033
FAX: 303-866-4077
Email: tom.hart@state.co.us

CONNECTICUT —
Use HUD address above.

DELAWARE — Use HUD address above.

DISTRICT OF COLUMBIA
(Washington, D.C.) — Use HUD address above.

FLORIDA
Mr. Edward D. Broyles, Bureau Chief
Bureau of Mobile Homes & RV
Division of Motor Vehicles
2900 Apalachee Parkway, Room A-129
Tallahassee, FL 32399-0640
PH: 850-488-8600
FAX: 850-488-7053
Email: MHRV@hsmv.state.fl.us
Designee: Chuck Smith, Program Manager

GEORGIA
Mr. Chris Stephens, Asst. State Fire Marshal
Manufactured Housing Division
State Fire Marshal's Office
#2 Martin Luther King Jr. Dr, #620 West Tower
Atlanta, GA 30334
PH: 404-656-3687 or 404-656-9498
FAX: 404-657-6971
Email: manhousing@mail.oci.state.ga.us
Designee: Joe Hall (IPIA)

HAWAII — Use HUD address above.

IDAHO
Mr. Dave Munroe, Administrator Street Address:
Division of Building Safety — Building Bureau
P.O. Box 83720,Boise, ID 83720-0060
277 N. Sixth Street, Suite #100
Boise, ID 83702-7720
PH: 208-334-3896
FAX: 208-334-2683
Email: trodgers@dbs.state.id.us

ILLINOIS — Use HUD address above.

INDIANA
Ms. Richelle (Shelly) Wakefield, CBO
Administrator. Codes Enforcement Division
Indiana Government Center South
402 W. Washington, Street, Room W-246
Indianapolis, IN 46204
PH: 317-232-1407
FAX: 317-232-0146
Email: rwakefield@sema.state.in.us

IOWA

VACANT, State Fire Marshal
Department of Public Safety
Iowa State Building Code Bureau
621 E. Second Street
Des Moines, IA 50309-1831
PH: 515-281-5821
FAX: 515-242-6299
Email: linklett@dps.state.ia.us
Designee: David Linkletter
PH: 641-342-3050
FAX: 641-342-4653

KANSAS — Use HUD address above.

KENTUCKY

Mr. Harry Rucker, Chief
Manufactured Housing Division
Dept of Housing, Building & Construction
1049 US 127 South Building — Annex 4
Frankfort, KY 40601-4322
PH: 502-564-3626
DD: 502-564-4018
FAX: 502-564-4011
Email: harry.rucker@mail.state.ky.us

LOUISIANA

Mr. Michael Cammarosano, Administrative Dir.
Manufactured Housing Division
State Fire Marshal's Office
5150 Florida Boulevard
Baton Rouge, LA 70806-4125
PH: 225-925-4911 or 800-256-5452
FAX: 225-925-3699
Email: mcammaro@dps.state.la.us

MAINE

Ms. Anne Head, Executive Director
Manufactured Housing Board
Dept. of Professional & Financial Regulation
35 State House Station
Augusta, ME 04333-0035
PH: 207-624-8603 or 207-624-8612
FAX: 207-624-8637
Email: anne.l.head@state.me.us
Designee: Diane Sawyer

MARYLAND

Mr. James Hanna, Director
Dept of Housing & Community Development
Maryland Code Administration
100 Community Place
Crownsville, MD 21032-2023
PH: 410-514-7220
FAX: 410-987-8902
Email: hanna@dhcd.state.md.us
Designee: Kanti Patel or Charles Cook

MASSACHUSETTS —
Use HUD address above.

MICHIGAN

Mr. Richard A. VanderMolen
Director, Manufactured Housing
and Land Development Division
P.O. Box 30703
Lansing, MI 48909-8203
PH: 517-241-6300
FAX: 517-241-6301
Email: richard.a.vandermolen@cis.state.mi.us
Designee: Kevin DeGroat

MINNESOTA

Mr. Thomas Joachim, Director
MN Building Codes & Standards Division
Dept of Administration
Manufactured Structures Section
121 7th Place E., Suite 408
St. Paul, MN 55101-2181
PH: 651-296-4639
FAX: 651-297-1973
Email: randy.vogt@state.mn.us
Designee: Randy Vogt
PH: 651-296-9927

MISSISSIPPI

Mr. Millard Mackey, Chief Deputy Street
    Address:
Manufactured Housing Division
State Fire Marshal's Office
550 High Street, Suite 706
Jackson, MS 39201
P.O. Box 79
Jackson, MS 39205-0079
PH: 601-359-1061
FAX: 601-359-1076
Emails: genehumphrey@mid.state.ms.us
Designee: Gene Humphrey, Dep. Fire Marshal
firemarshal@mid.state.ms.us

MISSOURI

Mr. Steve Jungmeyer, Director
Dept of Manufactured Housing, & Modular
   Units
Missouri Public Service Commission
P.O. Box 360
301 West High Street, Rm 530
Jefferson City, MO 65102
PH: 573-751-7119 or 1-800-819-3180
FAX: 573-522-2509
Email: sjungmey@mail.state.mo.us
Designee: Wess Henderson, Administrator

MONTANA — Use HUD address above.

NEBRASKA

Mr. Mark Luttich, Department Director
Nebraska Public Service Commission
Housing & Recreational Vehicle Department
P.O. Box 94927
300 The Atrium; 1200 N Street
Lincoln, NE 68509-4927
PH: 402-471-0518
FAX: 402-471-7709
Email: mluttich@mail.state.ne.us
Designee: Kent Priby 402-471-0514

NEVADA

Ms. Renee Diamond, Administrator
Department of Business & Industry
Manufactured Housing Division
2501 E. Sahara Avenue, Suite 204
Las Vegas, NV 89104-4137
PH: 702-486-4135 or (DD) 702-486-4278
FAX: 702-486-4309
Email: rdiamond@govmail.state.nv.us
Designee: Gary Childers

NEW HAMPSHIRE —

Use HUD address above.

NEW JERSEY

Mr. Paul Sachdeva, Manager
NJ Division of Codes & Standards
Dept. of Community Affairs
P.O. Box 816
101 S. Broad Street
Trenton, NJ 08625-0816
PH: 609-984-7820
FAX: 609-984-7952

NEW MEXICO

Mr. Robert M. Unthank, Program Manager
Manufactured Housing Division
Regulation & Licensing Department
725 St. Michael's Drive
Santa Fe, NM 87505-7605
PH: 505-827-7070 or (DD) 505-827-7028
FAX: 505-827-7074
Email: john.wilson@state.nm.us
mike.unthank@state.nm.us
Designee: John Wilson (SAA)

NEW YORK

Mr. Arnold Byrd, Administrator
Manufactured Housing Unit
Department of State
Code Division
41 State Street, Room 1130
Albany, NY 12207-2839
PH: 518-474-4073 or (DD) 518-473-8901
FAX: 518-486-4487
Email: abyrd@dos.state.ny.us

NORTH CAROLINA

Mr. C. Patrick Walker, Deputy Commissioner
Manufactured Building Division
Department of Insurance
410 N. Boylan Avenue
Raleigh, NC 27603-1212
PH: 919-733-3901
Consumer Assistant Line: 800-587-2716
FAX: 919-715-9693
Email: dgoins@mail.doi.state.nc.us
Designee: David Goins, Administrator
PH: 252-754-2195
FAX: 252-754-2516

NORTH DAKOTA —

Use HUD address above.

OHIO — Use HUD address above.

OKLAHOMA —

Use HUD address above.

OREGON

Mr. Joseph A. Brewer, III, Administrator
Department of Consumer & Business Services
Building Codes Division
MAIL: P. O. Box 14470
1535 Edgewater Drive, NW
Salem, OR 97309-0404
PH: 503-378-4133
FAX: 503-378-2322
Email: joe.a.brewer@state.or.us
Designee: Dana Roberts
PH: 503-378-8450
FAX: 503-378-4101

PENNSYLVANIA

Mr. John F. Boyer, Jr.
Chief, Manufactured Housing Division
Community Development & Housing Office
Department of Community & Economic
Development
Forum Building, #372
Harrisburg, PA 17120-01555
PH: 717-720-7413
FAX: 717-783-4663
Email: john_boyer@dced.state.pa.us
Designee: Mark Conte

RHODE ISLAND

Mr. Joseph Cirillo, Commissioner
Building Code Commission
State of Rhode Island
Department of Administration
One Capitol Hill
Providence, RI 02908-5859
PH: 401-222-3033
FAX: 401-222-2599
Email: elaineg@gw.doa.state.ri.us
dandedentro@doa.state.ri.us
Designee: Richard Mancini
PH: 401-222-6332

SOUTH CAROLINA

Mr. Gary Wiggins, Administrator
SC Dept of Labor, Licensing & Regulation
Real Estate & Bldg. Code Professions
110 Centerview Dr., Suite 102
Columbia, SC 29211-1329
PH: 803-896-4682 or 803-896-4688
FAX: 803-896-4814
Email: wigginsg@mail.llr.state.sc.us

SOUTH DAKOTA

Mr. Daniel R. Carlson, State Fire Marshal
Office of State Fire Marshal
Dept of Commerce & Regulations
118 West Capitol Avenue
Pierre, SD 57501-5070
PH: 605-773-3562
FAX: 605-773-6631
Email: paul.merriman@state.sd.us
Designee: Paul Merriman

TENNESSEE

Mr. Tim Garrington, Director
Codes & Standards, Div of Fire Prevention
Department of Commerce & Insurance
500 James Robertson Parkway
Nashville, TN 37243-1162
PH: 615-741-6246
FAX: 615-741-1583
Email: tgarrington@mail.state.tn.us
Designee: Tom Battle (IPIA)
PH: 615-741-7048

TEXAS

Ms. Bobbie Hill, Administrator
Manufactured Housing
TX Dept of Housing & Community Affairs
P. O. Box 12489
Austin, TX 78711-2489
PH: 512-475-3983 or 800-500-7074
FAX: 512-475-4250
Email: bhill@tdhca.state.tx.us
Designee: James Galbreath

UTAH

Mr. Daniel S. Jones, Director
Construction Trades Bureau
Div of Occupational & Professional Licensing
Department of Commerce
P. O. Box 146741
160 E. 300 South
Salt Lake City, UT 84114-6741
PH: 801-530-6720 or (DD) 801-530-6720
FAX: 801-530-6511
Email: dsjones@br.state.ut.us
Designee: Ed Short

VERMONT — Use HUD address above.

VIRGINIA

Mr. Curtis McIver, Associate Director
Manufactured Housing Office
Dept of Housing & Community Development
Jackson Center, 501 N. Second Street
Richmond, VA 23219-1321
PH: 804-371-7160
FAX: 804-371-7092
Email: cmciver@dhcd.state.va.us
Designee: Lorenzo Dyer

WASHINGTON

Ms. Teri Ramsauer, Manager
Office of Manufactured Housing
Dept of Community Trade & Economic
Development
906 Columbia St. SW
Olympia, WA 98504-8300
Ph: 360-586-6865 or 1-800-964-0852
FAX: 360-586-5880
Email: terir@cted.wa.gov

WEST VIRGINIA

Ms. Fran Cook, Administrator
West Virginia Division of Labor
Building Three, Room 319
Capitol Complex
Charleston, WV 25305
PH: 304-558-7890
FAX: 304-558-3797
Email: fcook@labor.state.wv.us

WISCONSIN

Mr. Ken Fiedler, Administrator
Manufactured Homes,
Safety & Building Division
Department of Commerce
P.O. Box 2538
Madison, WI 53707-2538
PH: 608-266-8577 (DD)
FAX: 608-267-9723
Email: kfiedler@commerce.state.wi.us

WYOMING — Use HUD address above.

Appendix C

LIST OF MOBILE HOME MANUFACTURERS

ALABAMA

BRILLIANT HOMES #1
P.O. BOX 216
HIGHWAY 129 N.
BRILLIANT, AL 35548
RICHARD THOMPSON
(205) 465-2334

BRILLIANT/CARRIAGE HOMES
P.O. BOX 69
GUIN, AL 35563
GENERAL MANAGER
(205) 468-3076

BRILLIANT/SILHOUETTE #3
BYLER ROAD
ROUTE 1, BOX 69
LYNN, AL 35575
GENERAL MANAGER

BUCCANEER HOMES #2 (CAVALIER)
P.O. BOX 389
WINFIELD, AL 35594
CHARLES DEMPSEY
(205) 487-3135

BUCCANEER HOMES #3 (CAVALIER)
P.O. BOX 386
WINFIELD, AL 35594
CHARLES DEMPSEY
(205) 487-5135

BUCCANEER HOMES OF AL (CAVALIER)
P.O. BOX 1418
INDUSTRIAL PARK ROAD
HAMILTON, AL 35570
GENERAL MANAGER
(205) 921-3135

CAVALIER HOMES #1
P.O. BOX 300
HIGHWAY 41 NORTH
ADDISON, AL 35540
GENERAL MANAGER
(205) 747-1575

CAVALIER HOMES #2
P.O. BOX 300
ADDISON, AL 35540
GENERAL MANAGER
(205) 747-1575

CAVALIER HOMES #3
P.O. BOX 540
AIRPORT ROAD
ADDISON, AL 35540
GENERAL MANAGER
(205) 747-1575

CHAMPION/GATEWAY HOMES
P.O. BOX 728
GUIN, AL 35563
GENERAL MANAGER
(205) 468-3191

CHANDELEUR HOMES #3
P.O. BOX 557
DENSON ROAD
BOAZ, AL 35957
GENERAL MANAGER
(205) 593-9225

CHANDELEUR HOMES, INC. #1
P.O. BOX 557
DENSON ROAD
BOAZ, AL 35957
GENERAL MANAGER
(205) 593-9225

CHANDELEUR HOMES, INC. #2
P.O. BOX 557
DENSON ROAD
BOAZ, AL 35957
GENERAL MANAGER
(205) 593-9225

CRIMSON HOMES/BEAR CREEK
P.O. BOX 1086
HWY 5 INDUSRIAL PARK
HALEYVILLE, AL 35565
TROY OLIVER
(205) 486-8111

CRIMSON INDUSTRIES, INC. #2
INDUSTRIAL PARK SOUTHWEST
HALEYVILLE, AL 35565
MR. SHOTTS
(205) 486-9222

CROWN HOUSING, INC.
P.O. BOX 97
HIGHWAY 172 NORTH
VINA, AL 35593
FRED COOPER
(205) 356-9378

CROWN HOUSING, INC.
P.O. BOX 159
HWY. 5 SOUTH
PHIL CAMPBELL, AL 35589
GENERAL MANAGER
(205) 993-8007

FRANKLIN HOMES, INC.
10655 HIGHWAY 43
RUSSELLVILLE, AL 35653
JERRY JAMES
(205) 332-4510

HOMES OF LEGEND, INC. #1
P.O. BOX 699
BOAZ, AL 35957
GENERAL MANAGER
(205) 593-9630

HOMES OF LEGEND, INC. #2
RIVER OAKS ROAD
P.O. BOX 699
BOAZ, AL 35957
GENERAL MANAGER
(205) 593-9630

HOMES OF LEGEND, INC. #3
P.O. BOX 699
BOAZ, AL 35957
GENERAL MANAGER
(205) 593-9630

HOMES OF LEGEND, INC. #4
P.O. BOX 699
BOAZ, AL 35957
(205) 593-1621

INDIES HOUSE, INC.
P.O. BOX 190
HIGHWAY 172
HACKLEBURG, AL 35564
THOMAS JAMES
(205) 935-3117

LIBERTY/WAVERLEE HOMES #2
680 WAVERLEE ROAD
SHOALS DIVISION
TUSCUMBIA, AL 35674
DICK PRESTAGE
(205) 381-4120

LIBERTY/WAVERLEE HOMES, INC.
P.O. BOX 1887 HWY. 278 EAST
BEDFORD INDUSTRIAL PARK
HAMILTON, AL 35570
STEVE LOGAN
(205) 921-1887

PALM HARBOR HOMES #16
BOAZ INDUSTRIAL BLVD.
P.O. BOX 640
BOAZ, AL 35957
GENERAL MANAGER
(205) 593-9193

PALM HARBOR HOMES, INC. #14
P.O. BOX 640
BOAZ INDUSTRIAL BLVD.
BOAZ, AL 35957
JAMES SAMPSON
(205) 593-9193

PATRIOT HOMES/SOUTHRIDGE #11
1871 BEXAR AVENUE EAST
HAMILTON, AL 35570
JOHN CALVERT
(205) 921-3144

PATRIOT HOMES/SOUTHRIDGE #5
1871 BEXAR AVENUE EAST
RT. 3 BOX 120 HWY. 278 EAST
HAMILTON, AL 35570
GENERAL MANAGER
(205) 921-3144

PINNACLE HOMES #1
P.O. BOX 550
HIGHWAY 278 EAST
SULLIGENT, AL 35586
JOEL LOGAN, PRES
(205) 698-8898

REDMAN HOMES, INC.
P.O. BOX 538
EASTABOGA, AL 36260
TOM SIMPSON
(205) 835-5881

RIVERCHASE HOMES (CAVALIER)
   INDUSTRIES
P.O. BOX 676
HALEYVILLE, AL 35565
GENERAL MANAGER
(205) 486-8165

SOUTHERN ENERGY HOMES #1
P.O. BOX 269
HIGHWAY 41 NORTH
ADDISON, AL 35540
GENERAL MANAGER
(205) 747-1544

SOUTHERN ENERGY HOMES #2
HIGHWAY 278 EAST
ADDISON, AL 35540
(205) 747-4191

SOUTHERN HOMES CO.
P.O. BOX 639
DOUBLE SPRINGS, AL 35553
GENERAL MANAGER
(205) 489-3433

SOUTHERN LIFESTYLE HOMES II
P.O. BOX 329
ADDISON, AL 35540
GENERAL MANAGER
(205) 747-1506

SOUTHERN LIFESTYLE HOMES, INC. #1
P.O. BOX 299
ADDISON, AL 35540
GENERAL MANAGER
(205) 747-1509

SPIRAL INDUSTRIES, INC.
P.O. BOX 130
HIGHWAY 43, SOUTH
RUSSELLVILLE, AL 35653
R.C. GODSEY
(205) 332-4530

SUNSHINE HOMES, INC. #1
P.O. BOX 507
RED BAY, AL 35582
GENERAL MANAGER
(205) 356-4428

SUNSHINE HOMES, INC. #2
P.O. BOX 507
509 6TH STREET WEST
RED BAY, AL 35582
GENERAL MANAGER
(205) 356-4427

ARKANSAS

SPIRIT HOMES/CENTRAL #3
P.O. BOX 1207
CONWAY, AR 72033
TROY FORD
(501) 327-2444

SPIRIT HOMES/CENTRAL #4
P.O. BOX 1207
HIGHWAY 286 & MCNUTT ROAD
CONWAY, AR 72032
GENERAL MANAGER
(501) 327-1108

ARIZONA

CAVCO III
1366 S. LITCHFIELD ROAD
BLDG. #6
GOODYEAR, AZ 85338
GENERAL MANAGER
(602) 925-6616

CAVCO INDUSTRIES
2502 W. DURANGO
PHOENIX, AZ 85009
GENERAL MANAGER
(602) 278-3554

CAVCO INDUSTRIES IV
1366 S. LITCHFIELD ROAD
BLDG. #6
GOODYEAR, AZ 85338
GENERAL MANAGER
(602) 925-6616

CAVCO INDUSTRIES, INC.
3502 W. LOWER BUCKEYE (PLANT)
2602 SOUTH 35TH AVE. (MAILING)
PHOENIX, AZ 85009
GENERAL MANAGER
(602) 484-0171

FLEETWOOD HOMES OF ARIZONA
6112 N. 56TH AVE.
GLENDALE, AZ 85301
GENERAL MANAGER
(602) 939-2600

PALM HARBOR HOMES #3
1108 WEST GILA BEND HIGHWAY
CASA GRANDE, AZ 85222
GENERAL MANAGER
(520) 836-1341

PALM HARBOR HOMES, INC. #02
309 S. PERRY
TEMPE, AZ 85281
GENERAL MANAGER
(602) 967-7877

REDMAN HOMES, INC.
400 EAST RAY ROAD
CHANDLER, AZ 85225
GENERAL MANAGER
(602) 963-8164

SCHULT HOMES #2
201 APACHE ROAD
P.O. BOX 908
BUCKEYE, AZ 85326
LIONEL CLARK
(602) 386-4495

SCHULT/MARLETTE HOMES
P.O. BOX 908
201 APACHE ROAD
BUCKEYE, AZ 85326
GENERAL MANAGER
(602) 386-4495

CALIFORNIA

CHAMPION HOME BUILDERS
P.O. BOX 429
840 PALM AVE.
LINDSAY, CA 93247
GENERAL MANAGER
(209) 562-4951

FLEETWOOD HOMES OF CA #08
P.O. BOX 4038
7007 JURUPA AVENUE
RIVERSIDE, CA 92504
GENERAL MANAGER
(909) 688-5353

FLEETWOOD HOMES OF CA #17
18 NORTH PIONEER AVE.
P.O. BOX 1308
WOODLAND, CA 95776
GENERAL MANAGER
(916) 662-9127

GOLDEN WEST/HOMES BY OAKWOOD
SOUTHERN CALIFORNIA DIV.
3100 N. PERRIS BLVD.
PERRIS, CA 92571
GEN. MGR. (CHINO & MORENO VLY.)
(714) 657-1611

HALLMARK-SOUTHWEST CORP.
25525 REDLANDS BLVD.
LOMA LINDA, CA 92354
GENERAL MANAGER
(714) 796-2561

SKYLINE CORP.
499 W. ESPLANADE
P.O. BOX 670
SAN JACINTO, CA 92583
GENERAL MANAGER
(909) 654-9321

SKYLINE CORP./BUDDY
P.O. BOX 1870
1720 EAST BEAMER STREET
WOODLAND, CA 95695
GENERAL MANAGER
(916) 666-0974

THE KARSTEN COMPANY
9998 OLD PLACERVILLE ROAD
SACRAMENTO, CA 95827
ANDY KARSTEN
(916) 363-2681

WESTERN HOMES/SILVERCREST
109 PIONEER AVENUE
WOODLAND, CA 95776
GENERAL MANAGER
(916) 662-9156

WESTERN/SILVERCREST HOMES
299 NORTH SMITH AVENUE
CORONA, CA 91720
GENERAL MANAGER
(909) 734-6610

COLORADO

CHAMPION/SUMMIT CREST HOMES
P.O. BOX 10
2221 CLAYTON LANE
BERTHOUD, CO 80513
GENERAL MANAGER
(303) 532-2632

GOLDEN WEST HOMES (OAKWOOD)
20870 HIGHWAY 34E
FORT MORGAN, CO 80701
PHILLIP CLARK
(907) 867-6454

DELAWARE

PAWNEE HOMES, INC. NANTICOKE)
ROUTE 13 SOUTH
P.O. BOX F
GREENWOOD, DE 19950
JOHN MERVINE, JR.
(302) 349-4561

FLORIDA

CHARIOT EAGLE, INC.
931 N.W. 37TH AVENUE
OCALA, FL 34475
TERRY HARRELL
(352) 629-7007

FLEETWOOD HOMES OF FL #70
P.O. BOX 1405
700 S. BARTOW ROAD
AUBURNDALE, FL 33823
GENERAL MANAGER
(813) 967-7575

FLEETWOOD HOMES OF FL #79
3804 SYDNEY ROAD
PLANT CITY, FL 33567
GENERAL MANAGER
(813) 754-1884

HOMES OF MERIT OF FL
P.O. BOX 1606
BARTOW AIR BASE BLDG. 121
BARTOW, FL 33830
GENERAL MANAGER
(941) 533-0593

HOMES OF MERIT OF FL
P.O. BOX 2097
HIGHWAY 100 EAST
LAKE CITY, FL 32056
GENERAL MANAGER
(904) 755-3073

JACOBSEN HOMES
P.O. BOX 368
901 FOURTH STREET NORTH
SAFETY HARBOR, FL 34695
GENERAL MANAGER
(813) 726-1138

LIBERTY HOMES, INC.
495 OAK ROAD
OCALA, FL 34472
GENERAL MANAGER
(800) 669-4981

NOBILITY HOMES #8
P.O. BOX 779
U.S. HIGHWAY 301 & SHOW ROAD
BELLVIEW, FL 34491
GENERAL MANAGER
(352) 245-5126

NOBILITY HOMES, INC. #01
P.O. BOX 1838
3741 S.W. 7TH STREET
OCALA, FL 32678
GENERAL MANAGER
(352) 732-6110

PALM HARBOR HOMES, INC.
605 S. FRONTAGE ROAD
PLANT CITY, FL 33566
GENERAL MANAGER
(813) 752-1368

PALM HARBOR HOMES, INC. #09
609 S. FRONTAGE ROAD
PLANT CITY, FL 33566
GENERAL MANAGER
(813) 752-1368

REDMAN HOMES, INC.
P.O. BOX "SS"
1602 INDUSTRIAL PARK
PLANT CITY, FL 33564
GENERAL MANAGER
(813) 754-1577

SKYLINE CORP./CAMERON
P.O. BOX 2168
OCALA, FL 33478
GENERAL MANAGER
(352) 622-5111

SKYLINE CORP./HOMETTE
P.O. BOX 2648
1230 S.W. 10TH STREET
OCALA, FL 34478
GENERAL MANAGER
(352) 629-7571

SKYLINE CORP./OAK SPRINGS
P.O. BOX 789
1714 SOUTHWEST 17TH STREET
OCALA, FL 34474
GENERAL MANAGER
(352) 629-7501

GEORGIA

BELLCREST HOMES #1
P.O. BOX 630
206 MAGNOLIA STREET
MILLEN, GA 30442
(912) 982-4000

BELLCREST HOMES #2
1458 OLD SYLVANIA ROAD
P.O. BOX 630
MILLEN, GA 30442
HILLER SPANN
(912) 982-4000

CLAYTON HOMES/WAYCROSS HOMES
ROUTE 4, BOX 284C
WAYCROSS, GA 31501
CHARLIE SHELL
(912) 283-6400

CRAFTMADE HOMES
P.O. BOX 466
SYLVESTER, GA 31791
CECIL RIGGS
(912) 776-2667

DESTINY HOMES 1 & 2 (OAKWOOD)
P.O. BOX 1766
INDUSTRIAL PARK DRIVE
MOULTRIE, GA 31768
GENERAL MANAGER
(912) 985-6100

DESTINY HOMES 3 & 4 (OAKWOOD)
P.O. BOX 1766
INDUSTRIAL PARK
MOULTRIE, GA 31768
(912) 985-6100

FLEETWOOD HOMES OF GA #05
P.O. BOX 272
NORTH INDUSTRIAL PARK
DOUGLAS, GA 31533
GENERAL MANAGER
(912) 384-1147

FLEETWOOD HOMES OF GA #35
P.O. BOX 810
AMBROSE HIGHWAY
BROXTON, GA 31519
GENERAL MANAGER
(912) 359-2392

FLEETWOOD HOMES OF GA #54
HIGHWAY 82 WEST
MAILING ADDRESS SAME AS FLWD35
PEARSON, GA 31642
GENERAL MANAGER
(912) 422-3434

FLEETWOOD HOMES OF GA #75
P.O. BOX 767
HWY. 32 W. IND. PARK
ALMA, GA 31510
GENERAL MANAGER
(912) 632-6789

FLEETWOOD/SPRING HILL #34
P.O. BOX 899
RAILROAD STREET
PEARSON, GA 31642
GENERAL MANAGER
(912) 422-7391

FLEETWOOD/SPRING HILL #34-02
FLEETWOOD AVE.
P.O. BOX 598
WILLACOOCHEE, GA 316500598
CHARLES WRYE
(912) 534-5960

FLEETWOOD/VALUHOMES
105 PIERCE CIRCLE
FITZGERALD, GA 31750
GENERAL MANAGER
(912) 424-0053

FLEETWOOD/WESTFIELD #07
P.O. BOX 828
HIGHWAY 441 NORTH
DOUGLAS, GA 31533
GENERAL MANAGER
(912) 384-1818

GENERAL MANUFACTURED
HOUSING, INC.
2255 INDUSTRIAL BLVD.
WAYCROSS, GA 31501
GENERAL MANAGER
(912) 285-5068

GRAND MANOR #1
270 DAVENPORT DRIVE
P.O. BOX 2657
THOMASVILLE, GA 31799
GENERAL MANAGER
(912) 228-0023

GRAND MANOR HOMES #2
P.O. BOX 2657
1025 CAMPBELL STREET
THOMASVILLE, GA 31799
MARCY SULLIVAN
(912) 226-5121

HOMESTEAD HOMES
P.O. BOX 1274
501 S. MIDWAY ROAD
CORDELE, GA 31015
GENERAL MANAGER
(912) 273-2021

HORTON HOMES
101 INDUSTRIAL BLVD.
EATONTON, GA 31024
GENERAL MANAGER
(706) 485-8506

HORTON HOMES
101 INDUSTRIAL BLVD.
EATONTON, GA 31024
GENERAL MANAGER

PALM HARBOR HOMES
1508 REDDING DR.
LAGRANGE, GA 30240
HUBERT BREWER
(706) 885-1200

PIONEER HOUSING SYSTEM, INC.
200 OCILLA HIGHWAY
FITZGERALD, GA 31750
GENERAL MANAGER
(800) 269-6630

PIONEER HOUSING SYSTEM, INC.
200 OCILLA HIGHWAY
FITZGERALD, GA 31750
GENERAL MANAGER
(800) 269-6630

REDMAN HOMES, INC.
P.O. BOX 319
U.S. 280 EAST
RICHLAND, GA 31825
GENERAL MANAGER
(912) 887-3386

SUNSTATE/PEACH STATE #2
P.O. BOX 615
I-75 9 & OLD QUITMAN-ADEL HWY.
ADEL, GA 31620
JERRY HORTON
(912) 896-4660

SUNSTATE/PEACH STATE HOMES
P.O. BOX 615
I-75 & OLD ADEL/QUITMAN HWY.
ADEL, GA 31620
GENERAL MANAGER
(912) 896-7420

SWEETWATER HOMES, INC.
309 EAST FOURTH STREET
OCILLA, GA 31774
GENERAL MANAGER
(912) 468-7164

IDAHO

CHAMPION HOMES/TAMARACK
P.O. BOX 190
ROUTE 3 OFF U.S. 95
WEISER, ID 83672
GENERAL MANAGER
(208) 549-1410

FLEETWOOD HOMES OF ID #04
P.O. BOX 1070
COMSTOCK AVENUE
NAMPA, ID 83653
GENERAL MANAGER
(208) 466-2438

FLEETWOOD HOMES OF ID #04-02
P.O. BOX 1070
NAMPA, ID 93651
(208) 466-2438

GUERDON INDUSTRIES, INC. #1
5556 FEDERAL WAY
BOISE, ID 83706
GENERAL MANAGER
(208) 345-5100

KIT MFG. CO. M-1
P.O. BOX 250
1124 GARBER
CALDWELL, ID 83606
GENERAL MANAGER
(208) 459-1575

NASHUA HOMES OF IDAHO
P.O. BOX 8449
5200 FEDERAL WAY
BOISE, ID 83707
GENERAL MANAGER
(208) 377-8862

INDIANA

CHAMPION HOME BUILDERS
P.O. BOX 57
N. PORTLAND ST.
RIDGEVILLE, IN 47380
GENERAL MANAGER
(317) 857-2561

COMMODORE CORP.
P.O. BOX 176
STATE ROAD 13 N.
SYRACUSE, IN 465670295
GENERAL MANAGER
(219) 457-3154

COMMODORE/BROOKWOOD
1902 CENTURY DR.
P.O. BOX 729
GOSHEN, IN 46526
GENERAL MANAGER
(219) 534-3067

DUTCH HOUSING PLANT F
P.O. BOX 258
LAGRANGE, IN 46761
GENERAL MANAGER
(219) 463-3199

DUTCH HOUSING/LAGRANGE D
P.O. BOX 258
LAGRANGE, IN 46761
DAVE GANGOR
(616) 483-2353

DUTCH HOUSING/LAGRANGE E #5
P.O. BOX 258
LAGRANGE, IN 46761
GENERAL MANAGER
(219) 463-3199

DUTCH HOUSING/PLANT G
P.O. BOX 258
LAGRANGE, IN 46761
DAN THORNE
(219) 463-3199

FAIRMONT HOMES, INC. #01
502 S. OAKLAND STREET
NAPPANEE, IN 46550
GENERAL MANAGER
(219) 773-7941

FAIRMONT/EAST
502 SOUTH OAKLAND
NAPPANEE, IN 46550
GENERAL MANAGER
(219) 773-7941

FAIRMONT/FRIENDSHIP #02
502 S. OAKLAND
NAPPANEE, IN 46550
GENERAL MANAGER
(219) 773-7941

FAIRMONT/FRIENDSHIP IND. #01
502 SOUTH OAKLAND
NAPPANEE, IN 46550
GENERAL MANAGER
(219) 773-7941

FLEETWOOD HOMES #55-2
P.O. BOX 330
1850 STATE ROAD 8
GARRETT, IN 46738
GENERAL MANAGER
(219) 357-4134

FLEETWOOD HOMES #55-1
1119 FULLER DR.
GARRETT, IN 46738
KEN KESKA
(219) 357-5917

FOUR SEASONS HOUSING #1
105 14TH STREET
P.O. BOX 630
MIDDLEBURY, IN 46540
JIM MESSNER
(219) 825-9999

FOUR SEASONS HOUSING #2
P.O. BOX 630
105 14TH STREET
MIDDLEBURY, IN 46540
JIM MESSNER
(219) 825-9999

FOUR SEASONS HOUSING #4
104 14TH STREET
P.O. BOX 630
MIDDLEBURY, IN 46540
MARK FRANCIS
(219) 825-9999

HART HOUSING GROUP #2
STATE ROAD 19
66700 STATE ROAD 19
WAKARUSA, IN 46573
DOUG ROBBINS
(219) 862-4787

HI-TECH HOUSING, INC.
19319 COUNTY ROAD 8
BRISTOL, IN 46507
JEANETTE CAUSEY
(219) 848-5593

LIBERTY HOMES, INC.
P.O. BOX 308
STATE ROAD 13
SYRACUSE, IN 46567
GENERAL MANAGER
(219) 457-3121

PATRIOT HOMES #1
57420 C.R. 3 S.
ELKHART, IN 46517
GENERAL MANAGER
(219) 293-6507

PATRIOT HOMES/LINCOLN PARK
P.O. BOX 610
S.R. #5
SHIPSHEWANA, IN 46565
GENERAL MANAGER
(219) 768-4166

PATRIOT/ENERGYMATE HOMES
57420 C.R. 3 S.
ELKHART, IN 46517
GENERAL MANAGER
(219) 293-6507

PATRIOT/VICTORIAN HOMES PLT #4
P.O. BOX 707
FORMERLY VCTN01
MIDDLEBURY, IN 46540
GENERAL MANAGER
(219) 825-5841

REDMAN HOMES, INC.
P.O. BOX 95
TOPEKA, IN 46571
GENERAL MANAGER
(219) 593-2962

ROCHESTER HOMES
P.O. BOX 587
EAST LUCAS STREET
ROCHESTER, IN 46975
GENERAL MANAGER
(219) 223-4321

SCHULT HOMES
P.O. BOX 151
U.S. 20 WEST
MIDDLEBURY, IN 46540
GENERAL MANAGER

SCHULT HOMES PLANT #3
330 N. TOWER
ETNA GREEN, IN 46524
GENERAL MANAGER
(219) 858-2511

SHAMROCK HOMES
1201 WEST MARKLEY ROAD
PLYMOUTH, IN 46563
GENERAL MANAGER
(219) 935-5111

SKYLINE CORP./HILLCREST
P.O. BOX 217
STATE ROAD 15S
BRISTOL, IN 46507
GENERAL MANAGER
(219) 848-7621

SKYLINE HOMES ELKHART
P.O. BOX 1152
ELKHART, IN 46515
GENERAL MANAGER
(219) 522-8339

SKYLINE HOMES GOSHEN
P.O. BOX 435
U.S. HWY. 33 SOUTH
GOSHEN, IN 46526
GENERAL MANAGER
(219) 533-4179

SKYLINE/SUNSET RIDGE HOMES
P.O. BOX 100
STATE ROAD 9 NORTH
HOWE, IN 46546
GENERAL MANAGER
(219) 562-2341

THE NEW HOLLY PARK
51700 LOVEJOY DRIVE
MIDDLEBURY, IN 46540
THOMAS E. VAN METER
(219) 825-3700

THE NEW HOLLY PARK #2
51700 LOVEJOY DRIVE
MIDDLEBURY, IN 46540
TOM LIZZI
(219) 825-3700

KANSAS

LIBERTY HOMES
P.O. BOX 18
YODER, KS 67585
GENERAL MANAGER
(316) 663-2187

SCHULT HOMES
P.O. BOX 409
HIGHWAY K-18
PLAINVILLE, KS 67663
GENERAL MANAGER
(913) 434-4617

SKYLINE CORP.
P.O. BOX 311
920 WEST 2ND STREET
HALSTEAD, KS 67056
GENERAL MANAGER
(316) 835-2214

SKYLINE CORP./HOMETTE
P.O. BOX 719
HIGHWAY 77 NORTH
ARKANSAS CITY, KS 67005
GENERAL MANAGER
(316) 442-9060

KENTUCKY

FLEMING HOMES, INC.
P.O. BOX 426
FLEMING COUNTY INDUSTRIAL PARK
FLEMINGSBURG, KY 41041
GENERAL MANAGER

MID-AMERICA HOMES, INC.
HWY. 641 BY-PASS
P.O. BOX 490
BENTON, KY 42025
JEFF WEDAN
(502) 527-5006

LOUISIANA

SKYLINE CORP.
P.O. BOX 5811
1650 SWAN LAKE ROAD
BOSSIER CITY, LA 711115811
GENERAL MANGER
(318) 746-5001

MAINE

BURLINGTON HOMES OF MAINE
P.O. BOX 263
OXFORD, ME 04270
GENERAL MANAGER
(207) 539-4406

OXFORD HOMES #1
ROUTE 26 YORK STREET
OXFORD, ME 04270
GENERAL MANAGER
(207) 539-4412

MICHIGAN

DUTCH HOUSING, INC.
P.O. BOX 687
68956 U.S. 131 SOUTH
WHITE PIGEON, MI 49099
(616) 483-2333

DUTCH HOUSING/FORTUNE HOMES
P.O. BOX 199
WHITE PIGEON, MI 49099
(616) 483-7000

MINNESOTA

FRIENDSHIP HOMES OF MN
P.O. BOX 191
815 BUDD RD.
MONTEVIDEO, MN 56265
GENERAL MANAGER
(612) 269-6495

HIGHLAND MFGR., CO., INC.
1660 ROWE AVENUE
WORTHINGTON, MN 56187
GENERAL MANAGER
(507) 376-9460

SCHULT HOMES
P.O. BOX 399
201 INDUSTRIAL DRIVE
REDWOOD FALLS, MN 56283
GENERAL MANAGER
(507) 637-3555

THE HOMARK CO.
P.O. BOX 309
RED LAKE FALLS, MN 56750
GENERAL MANAGER

MISSOURI

AMERICAN FAMILY/TAYLOR MADE
  HOMES
P.O. BOX 438
HIGHWAY 71 NORTH
ANDERSON, MO 64831
GENERAL MANAGER
(417) 845-3311

FUQUA HOMES, INC.
P.O. BOX 354
RADIO HILL ROAD
BOONVILLE, MO 65233
GENERAL MANAGER
(816) 882-3411

MISSISIPPI

BELMONT HOMES #1
P.O. BOX 280
INDUSTRIAL PARK DRIVE
BELMONT, MS 38827
GERALD KENNEDY
(601) 454-9217

BELMONT HOMES #3
P.O. BOX 280
BELMONT, MS 38827
GENERAL MANAGER
(601) 454-9217

BELMONT HOMES #4
INDUSTRIAL DRIVE
P.O. BOX 280
BELMONT, MS 38827
GENERAL MANAGER
(601) 454-9217

BELMONT/DELTA HOMES
1322 INDUSTRIAL PARK DRIVE
CLARKSDALE, MS 38614
DAVE HOLCOMB
(601) 627-2588

CAPPAERT MANUFACTURED
HOUSING, INC.
P.O. BOX 820567
HWY. 61 SOUTH
VICKSBURG, MS 39182
LAMAR ROBERTS
(601) 636-5401

FLEETWOOD HMS. OF MS. 25-2
P.O. BOX 0
100 FLEETWOOD CIRCLE
LEXINGTON, MS 39095
GENERAL MANAGER
(601) 834-1005

FLEETWOOD HOMES #25-3
P.O. BOX 927
LEXINGTON, MS 39095
STEVE SMITH
(601) 834-4228

FLEETWOOD HOMES OF MS #25
BOX 927
100 FLEETWOOD CIRCLE
LEXINGTON, MS 39095
GENERAL MANAGER
(601) 834-1005

FREE STATE MOBILE HOMES #1
500 EASTVIEW DRIVE
P.O. BOX 6542
LAUREL, MS 39441
CARLTON BROWN
(601) 425-5999

FREE STATE MOBILE HOMES #2
P.O. BOX 6542
LAUREL, MS 39441
MIKE ELKINS
(601) 425-5999

GUERDON/MAGNOLIA (AMERICAN
HOMESTAR)
RTE. 6 BOX 33B
169 MAGNOLIA ROAD
VICKSBURG, MS 39180
BOB FLETCHER
(601) 636-6455

PINNACLE HOMES #2
60036 PUCKETT DRIVE
AMORY, MS 38821
(601) 257-1997

REDMAN HOMES, INC.
P.O. BOX 3309
10194 LORRAINE RD
GULFPORT, MS 39503
GENERAL MANAGER
(601) 896-8483

NORTH CAROLINA

BRIGADIER HOMES OF NC (CAVALIER)
P.O. BOX 1007
HIGHWAY 64 EAST
NASHVILLE, NC 27856
GENERAL MANAGER
(919) 459-7026

CHAMPION HOME BUILDERS
P.O. BOX 1148
OLD RIVER ROAD
LILLINGTON, NC 27546
GENERAL MANAGER
(910) 893-5713

CHAMPION HOMES/TITAN
P.O. BOX 1389
HIGHWAY 401 SOUTH
LILLINGTON, NC 27546
GENERAL MANAGER
(910) 893-2121

CLAYTON HOMES, INC.
2090 ROSS MILL ROAD
HENDERSON, NC 27536
GENERAL MANAGER
(919) 492-1300

CLAYTON/OXFORD HOMES, INC.
RTE. 3 BOX 111 D
OXFORD, NC 27565
GENERAL MANAGER
(919) 693-2225

CLAYTON/FISHER HOMES
P.O. BOX 1000
RICHFIELD, NC 28137
GENERAL MANAGER
(704) 463-1341

CRESTLINE HOMES
ROUTE 3 BOX 67
LAURINBURG, NC 28352
GENERAL MANAGER
(919) 276-0195

FLEETWOOD HOMES #46
P.O. BOX 1187
ROUTE 6 HWY. 74 WEST
LUMBERTON, NC 28359
JIMMY HOLMES
(910) 671-4999

FLEETWOOD HOMES OF NC #41
P.O. BOX 818
EAST RAILROAD ST.
PEMBROKE, NC 28372
GENERAL MANAGER
(910) 521-9731

FLEETWOOD HOMES OF NC #41-2
P.O. BOX 818
PEMBROKE, NC 28372
GENERAL MANAGER
(910) 521-9731

FLEETWOOD HOMES OF NC #56
P.O. BOX 270
U.S. HWY. 115 SOUTH AT TIMBER
   RD.
MOORESVILLE, NC 28115
GENERAL MANAGER
(704) 663-7023

FLEETWOOD HOMES OF NC #69-1
P.O. BOX 1155
455 LUCY GARRETT ROAD
ROXBORO, NC 27573
GENERAL MANAGER
(919) 597-3602

GOLD MEDAL HOMES/R-ANELL
P.O. BOX 1009
HWY. 16, SOUTH
DENVER, NC 28037
GENERAL MANAGER
(704) 483-0901

HEARTLAND HOMES/AMERICAN
   HOMESTAR
P.O. BOX 1479
STATE ROUTE 1216
HENDERSON, NC 27536
(919) 492-1151

HOMES BY OAKWOOD #1
P.O. BOX 248
HIGHWAY 52 RHEA STREET
RICHFIELD, NC 28137
GENERAL MANAGER
(704) 463-7333

HOMES BY OAKWOOD #2
P.O. BOX 248
HIGHWAY 52 RHEA STREET
RICHFIELD, NC 28137
GENERAL MANAGER
(704) 463-7333

HOMES BY OAKWOOD #3
P.O. BOX 825
U.S. HWY. 1 NORTH
PINEBLUFF, NC 28373
(704) 463-7333

HOMES BY OAKWOOD #5
P.O. BOX 608
VICOUNT ROAD
ROCKWELL, NC 28138
GENERAL MANAGER
(704) 279-7287

HOMES BY OAKWOOD #7
508 PALMER RD.
ROCKWELL, NC 28138
GENERAL MANAGER
(704) 463-7333

LIBERTY HOMES, INC.
P.O. BOX 821
RT. 1, BOX 632
STATESVILLE, NC 28677
GENERAL MANAGER
(704) 878-2001

MANSION HOMES, INC.
P.O. BOX 39
PLANK ROAD
ROBBINS, NC 27325
GENERAL MANAGER
(910) 948-2141

PALM HARBOR/MASTERPIECE
2000 STERLING DRIVE
ALBEMARLE, NC 28001
GENERAL MANAGER
(704) 983-6464

PALM HARBOR/VILLA PARK EAST
2519 N.W. 2ND AVE.
P.O. BOX 583
SILER CITY, NC 27344
GENERAL MANAGER
(919) 663-2182

R-ANELL CUSTOM HOMES
P.O. BOX 428
ROUTE 16
DENVER, NC 28037
GENERAL MANAGER
(704) 483-5511

REDMAN HOMES, INC.
P.O. BOX 2686
HIGHWAY 421 & COXMILL ROAD
SANFORD, NC 27330
GENERAL MANAGER
(919) 258-3321

REDMAN HOMES, INC.
P.O. BOX 905
RT. 2 BOX 71 AIRBASE ROAD
MAXTON, NC 28364
GENERAL MANAGER
(910) 844-5055

SKYLINE CORP./HOMETTE
P.O. BOX 845
BETHEL CHURCH ROAD
MOCKSVILLE, NC 27028
GENERAL MANAGER
(704) 634-3511

SOUTHERN ENERGY/IMPERIAL
   HOMES OF NC
2100 STERLING DRIVE
(CORP-SOUTHERN ENERGY)
ALBEMARLE, NC 28001
GENERAL MANAGER
(704) 983-5292

NEBRASKA

ATLANTIC HOMES
P.O. BOX 148
NORTH HIGHWAY 14
CENTRAL CITY, NE 68826
MR. DONALD G. COTNER
(308) 946-3021

CHAMPION HOME BUILDERS
P.O. BOX 585
3200 ENTERPRISE AVENUE
YORK, NE 68467
GENERAL MANAGER
(402) 362-4455

CHAMPION/SUPERIOR HOUSING
P.O. BOX 509
1914 SOUTH GRANT AVENUE
YORK, NE 68467
GENERAL MANAGER
(402) 362-1200

CHIEF IND./BONNAVILLA
P.O. BOX 127
HIGHWAY 34 INDUSTRIAL RD.
AURORA, NE 68818
GENERAL MANAGER
(402) 694-5250

CHIEF/BONNAVILLA #2
ROUTE 1, BOX 6302
YORK, NE 68467
BOB PHILLIPS
(402) 363-7460

GUERDON IND./MAGNOLIA
P.O. BOX 657
982 RUNDELL ROAD
GERING, NE 69341
GENERAL MANAGER
(308) 436-3131

NEW MEXICO

CAVCO INDUSTRIES OF
   NEW MEXICO
80 DON LUIS TRUJILLO BLVD.
BELEN, NM 87002
(505) 861-3995

NEW YORK

CHAMPION HOMES/TITAN
BOX 56
ROUTE 12
SANGERFIELD, NY 13455
GENERAL MANAGER
(315) 841-4122

OHIO

MANUFACTURED HOUSING
   ENTERPRISES
09302 STATE ROUTE #6
BRYAN, OH 43506
GENERAL MANAGER
(419) 636-4511

PALM HARBOR/VILLA PARK EAST
P.O. BOX 38
ROUTE 22 EAST
SABINA, OH 45169
GENERAL MANAGER
(513) 584-2401

SKYLINE CORP.
580 MILL STREET N.W.
SUGARCREEK, OH 446819561
GENERAL MANAGER
(330) 852-2483

OKLAHOMA

ELLIOTT HOMES, INC. #2
1000 INDUSTRIAL ROAD
P.O. BOX 120
MADILL, OK 73446
GENERAL MANAGER
(405) 795-9921

ELLIOTT HOMES/DUNCAN
930 BOREN DRIVE
DUNCAN, OK 73534
PETE HOGSTAD, GM
(405) 255-8605

ELLIOTT MOBILE HOMES
P.O. BOX 209
EAST D STREET & HWY. 81
WAURIKA, OK 73573
GENERAL MANAGER
(405) 228-3572

OREGON

FLEETWOOD HOMES OF OR #48
P.O. BOX 628
2655 PROGRESS WAY
WOODBURN, OR 97071
GENERAL MANAGER
(503) 981-3136

FLEETWOOD HOMES OF OR #48-3
P.O. BOX 628
WOODBURN, OR 97071
GENERAL MANAGER
(503) 981-3136

FUQUA HOMES, INC.
P.O. BOX 5579
MURRAY ROAD
BEND, OR 97708
GENERAL MANAGER
(503) 382-4252

GOLDEN WEST HOMES #1
 (OAKWOOD)
2445 S. PACIFIC BLVD.
ALBANY, OR 97321
GENERAL MANAGER
(541) 926-8631

GUERDON INDUSTRIES, INC.
P.O. BOX 537
1200 WILCO ROAD
STAYTON, OR 97383
GENERAL MANAGER
(503) 769-6333

HOMEBUILDERS NORTHWEST, INC.
1650 INDUSTRIAL DRIVE
SALEM, OR 97305
GENERAL MANAGER
(503) 391-8936

LIBERTY HOMES, INC. #01
P.O. BOX 188
E. END OF SHERIDAN ROAD
SHERIDAN, OR 97378
GENERAL MANAGER
(503) 843-2255

PALM HARBOR HOMES #20
3737 PALM HARBOR DRIVE
MILLERSBURG, OR 97321
GENERAL MANAGER
(503) 926-2626

REDMAN HOMES, INC.
1204 MILL STREET
SILVERTON, OR 97381
GENERAL MANAGER
(503) 873-6381

SCHULT/MARLETTE HOMES
P.O. BOX 910
400 WEST ELM STREET
HERMISTON, OR 97838
GENERAL MANAGER
(541) 567-5546

SKYLINE CORP./HOMETTE
P.O. BOX 388
550 W. BOOTH BEND ROAD
MCMINNVILLE, OR 97128
GENERAL MANAGER
(503) 472-3181

WESTERN HOMES/SILVERCREST
P.O. BOX 565
2550 PROGRESS WAY
WOODBURN, OR 97071
GENERAL MANAGER
(503) 981-8808

PENNSYLVANIA

ASTRO MFGR. (CAVALIER INDUSTRIES)
P.O. BOX 189
ROUTE 66
SHIPPENSVILLE, PA 16254
GENERAL MANAGER
(814) 226-6822

CASTLE HOUSING OF PA
BOYLE MEMORIAL DRIVE
P.O. BOX 609
KNOX, PA 16232
GARY WILKERSON
(814) 797-1176

CHAMPION HOMES/ATLANTIC
P.O. BOX 343
OFF ROUTE 220
CLAYSBURG, PA 16625
GENERAL MANAGER
(814) 239-5121

COLONY FACTORY CRAFTED HOMES
P.O. BOX 310
RT. 66N-EXIT 8 I-80
SHIPPENVILLE, PA 16254
GENERAL MANAGER
(814) 226-9590

COMMODORE CORP.
P.O. BOX 349
RTE. 66 N. OFF INTERSTATE 80
CLARION, PA 16214
GENERAL MANAGER
(814) 226-9210

COMMODORE/MANORWOOD HOMES
ROUTE 443
P.O. BOX 169
PINE GROVE, PA 17963
ROBERT KEEPEL
(717) 345-0387

FLEETWOOD HOMES OF PA #22-2
60 INDUSTRIAL ROAD
P.O. BOX 530
ELIZABETHTOWN, PA 17022
GENERAL MANAGER
(717) 367-8222

LIBERTY HOMES, INC.
P.O. BOX 129
21 S. GROFFDALE ROAD
LEOLA, PA 17540
GENERAL MANAGER
(717) 656-2381

NEW ERA BUILDING SYSTEMS, INC.
451 SOUTHERN AVE.
P.O. BOX 269
STRATTANVILLE, PA 16258
MANAGER
(814) 764-5581

PINE GROVE MFG. HOMES, INC.
P.O. BOX 128
ROUTE 443
PINE GROVE, PA 17963
(717) 345-2011

REDMAN HOMES, INC.
P.O. BOX 428
GARDEN SPOT ROAD
EPHRATA, PA 17522
GENERAL MANAGER
(717) 733-7941

RITZ-CRAFT CORP.
P.O. BOX 70
50 N. 13TH STREET
MIFFLINBURG, PA 17844
GENERAL MANAGER
(717) 966-1053

SCHULT/CREST HOMES
30 INDUSTRIAL PARK ROAD
MILTON, PA 17847
GENERAL MANAGER
(717) 742-8521

SCHULT/MARLETTE HOMES
30 INDUSTRIAL PARK ROAD
P.O. BOX 947
LEWISTOWN, PA 17044
GENERAL MANAGER
(717) 248-3947

SKYLINE CORP./HILLCREST
99 HORSESHOE ROAD
LEOLA, PA 17540
GENERAL MANAGER
(717) 656-2071

SKYLINE HOMES, INC.
495 N. READING ROAD
EPHRATA, PA 17522
JOE BONACUSE
(717) 733-4171

SOUTH CAROLINA

GENERAL/LAMAR HOUSING
P.O. BOX 1080
206 RAILROAD AVENUE
LAMAR, SC 29069
ED BURTON
(803) 326-1300

MASCOT HOMES
P.O. BOX 127
HIGHWAY 176
GRAMLING, SC 29348
GENERAL MANAGER
(864) 472-2041

SOUTH DAKOTA

MEDALLION HOMES
P.O. BOX 1024
WEST HIGHWAY 212
WATERTOWN, SD 57201
GENERAL MANAGER
(605) 886-3270

TENNESSEE

CHAMPION HOMES/ATLANTIC
P.O. BOX 100
ATLANTIC AVENUE
HENRY, TN 38231
GENERAL MANAGER
(901) 243-2041

CLAYTON HOMES/ARDMORE
P.O. BOX 246
CLAYTON ROAD
ARDMORE, TN 38449
GENERAL MANAGER
(615) 427-6151

CLAYTON HOMES/HALLS DIV.
3938 FOUNTAIN VALLEY
KNOXVILLE, TN 37918
GENERAL MANAGER
(615) 922-9075

CLAYTON HOMES/MAYNARDVILLE
164 RACCOON VALLEY RD.
MAYNARDVILLE, TN 37807
GENERAL MANAGER
(615) 992-3851

CLAYTON HOMES/RUTLEDGE
ROUTE 2 BOX 415
ROUTE 2 HIGHWAY 11-W
RUTLEDGE, TN 37861
GENERAL MANAGER
(615) 828-5771

CLAYTON HOMES/SAVANNAH
ROUTE 7 BOX 271
AIRPORT ROAD
SAVANNAH, TN 38372
GENERAL MANAGER
(901) 925-1902

CLAYTON HOMES/SAVANNAH #2
ROUTE 7 BOX 271
AIRPORT ROAD
SAVANNAH, TN 38372
DAVID STEWART
(901) 925-1902

CLAYTON HOMES/WHITE PINE
2215 WALNUT STREET
WHITE PINE, TN 37890
JERRY L. WILLIAMS
(615) 674-7000

CLAYTON/APPALACHIA HOMES
1420 MOUNTAIN ROAD
ANDERSONVILLE, TN 37705
RONNIE ROBERTSON
(615) 494-7800

FLEETWOOD HMS. OF TN #26-2
4011 FLEETWOOD DR.
P.O. BOX 559
WESTMORELAND, TN 37186
(615) 644-5400

FLEETWOOD HOMES #27-2
739 HIGHWAY 52 BY-PASS WEST
LAFAYETTE, TN 37083
BILL GRAVES
(615) 666-0027

FLEETWOOD HOMES OF TN #26-1
P.O. BOX 559
PLEASANT GROVE ROAD
WESTMORELAND, TN 37186
GENERAL MANAGER
(615) 644-2211

FLEETWOOD HOMES OF TN #27
1500 AIRPORT ROAD
P.O. BOX 1139
GALLATIN, TN 37066
GENERAL MANAGER
(615) 451-0027

GILES INDUSTRIES OF TAZEWELL #1
405 SOUTH BROAD STREET
NEW TAZEWELL, TN 37825
GENERAL MANAGER
(423) 626-7243

GILES INDUSTRIES OF TAZEWELL #2
405 SOUTH BROAD STREET
NEW TAZEWELL, TN 37825
GENERAL MANAGER
(423) 626-7243

HOMES BY OAKWOOD #12
1860 MINES ROAD
PULASKI, TN 38478
GENERAL MANAGER
(615) 424-0733

LOVING HOMES, INC.
280 MEMORIAL LANE
JACKSBORO, TN 37757
RALPH GRANT
(615) 566-7400

NORRIS INC. #01
P.O. BOX 96
HWY. 11 WEST
BEAN STATION, TN 37708
GENERAL MANAGER
(423) 993-3343

NORRIS, INC. #02
P.O. BOX 99
HWY. 11 WEST
BEAN STATION, TN 37708
GENERAL MANAGER
(423) 993-7905

TEXAS

AMERICAN HOMESTAR OF
  BURLESON, INC.
320 N. BURLESON BLVD.
BURLESON, TX 76028
GENERAL MANAGER
(817) 295-8108

AMERICAN HOMESTAR/OAK
  CREEK HOMES
4805 E. LOOP 820 SOUTH
FORT WORTH, TX 76119
GENERAL MANAGER
(817) 478-5551

ARMSTRONG HOMES CORP.
P.O. BOX 1724
JACKSONVILLE, TX 75766
(214) 586-6555

CAVALIER TOWN AND COUNTRY #1
P.O. BOX 161727
4801 MARK IV PARKWAY
FT. WORTH, TX 76161
GENERAL MANAGER
(817) 740-9030

CAVALIER TOWN AND COUNTRY #2
6001 COLUMBIA STREET
MINERAL WELLS, TX 76067
LARRY BELL
(817) 325-2151

CAVALIER TOWN AND COUNTRY #3
216 NORTH OHIO STREET
P.O. BOX 2045
GRAHAM, TX 76450
(940) 549-2267

CLAYTON HOMES
333 AUSTIN STREET
BONHAM, TX 75418
GENERAL MANAGER
(903) 583-1949

CLAYTON HOMES
P.O. BOX 1310
2600 MAIN STREET
SULPHUR SPRINGS, TX 75483
JIM JUSTICE
(903) 439-0242

CLAYTON HOMES OF WACO TX #1
6800 IMPERIAL DRIVE
WACO, TX 76712
GENERAL MANAGER
(817) 776-6635

CLAYTON HOMES OF WACO TX #2
7001 IMPERIAL DRIVE
WACO, TX 76712
GENERAL MANAGER
(817) 772-1808

CREST RIDGE HOMES #1
P.O. BOX 1618
BRECKENRIDGE, TX 76424
GENERAL MANAGER
(817) 559-8211

CREST RIDGE HOMES #2
P.O. BOX 1618
1000 INDUSTRIAL BLVD.
BRECKENRIDGE, TX 76424
JOHN DRAKE
(817) 559-8211

FLEETWOOD HOMES OF TEXAS #66
2400 BURKBURNETT ROAD
WICHITA FALLS, TX 76304
PAUL WIEST
(817) 723-2777

FLEETWOOD HOMES OF TEXAS #86-2
1313 INDUSTRIAL PARK ROAD
P.O. BOX 1597
BELTON, TX 76513
GENERAL MANAGER
(817) 933-7044

FLEETWOOD HOMES OF TX #12-2
2800 E. INDUSTRIAL BLVD.
WACO, TX 76705
(817) 867-6377

FLEETWOOD HOMES OF TX #12-3
2801 GHOLSON ROAD
P.O. BOX 154488 (ZIP 76715)
WACO, TX 76705
GENERAL MANAGER
(817) 799-6206

FLEETWOOD HOMES OF TX #12N-1
P.O. BOX 154488
WACO, TX 76715
GENERAL MANAGER
(817) 799-6206

FLEETWOOD HOMES OF TX #84-1
P.O. BOX 21508
WACO, TX 76702
GENERAL MANAGER
(817) 751-1290

FLEETWOOD HOMES OF TX #86-1
520 SPARTA ROAD
P.O. BOX 1547
BELTON, TX 76513
TOM STONEBURNER
(254) 933-2384

GREAT TEXAS HOMES
555 GELLHORN
P.O. BOX 7064
HOUSTON, TX 77248
GENERAL MANAGERR
(713) 674-3163

HOMES BY OAKWOOD #10
4101 SOUTH 1-45
ENNIS, TX 75119
CHARLIE JORDAN
(972) 875-8155

HOMES BY OAKWOOD #8
1020 INDUSTRIAL LOOP
HILLSBORO, TX 76645
GENERAL MANAGER
(817) 582-2322

HOMES BY OAKWOOD #9
1020 INDUSTRIAL LOOP
HILLSBORO, TX 76645
GENERAL MANAGER
(817) 582-2322

PALM HARBOR HOMES #17
401 S. BURLESON BLVD.
BURLESON, TX 76028
GENERAL MANAGER
(817) 495-8464

PALM HARBOR HOMES, INC. #05
830 BASTROP HIGHWAY
AUSTIN, TX 78741
GENERAL MANAGER
(512) 385-1110

PALM HARBOR HOMES, INC. #07
830 BASTROP HIGHWAY
AUSTIN, TX 78741
GENERAL MANAGER
(512) 385-1110

PALM HARBOR/MASTERPIECE
  HOUSING
P.O. BOX 10
IH 35 SOUTH COUNTY ROAD 210
BUDA, TX 78610
GENERAL MANAGER
(512) 312-0621

PALM HARBOR/MASTERPIECE HSG.
6901 BOWMAN ROBERTS ROAD
FT. WORTH, TX 76179
GENERAL MANAGER
(817) 237-7205

PATRIOT HOMES OF TEXAS #10
1001 W. LOOP 340
WACO, TX 76712
GENERAL MANAGER
(817) 772-3336

PATRIOT HOMES OF TEXAS #8
1001 WEST LOOP 340
WACO, TX 76712
GENERAL MANAGER
(817) 772-3336

REDMAN HOMES, INC.
P.O. BOX 1330
HIGHWAY 31 WEST
ATHENS, TX 75751
GENERAL MANAGER
(903) 675-5784

REDMAN HOMES, INC.
P.O. BOX 549
501 S. BURLESON BLVD.
BURLESON, TX 76028
GENERAL MANAGER
(817) 295-2267

SATURN HOUSING
2600 BONNAVILLA DRIVE
P.O. BOX 1598
GAINESVILLE, TX 76241
TOM UNDERWOOD
(817) 668-7100

SCHULT HOMES #1
P.O. BOX 571
2215 INDUSTRIAL DRIVE
NAVASOTA, TX 77868
GENERAL MANAGER
(409) 825-7501

SCHULT HOMES, INC. #2
P.O. BOX 571
2215 INDUSTRIAL DRIVE
NAVASOTA, TX 77868
GENERAL MANAGER
(409) 825-7501

SIGNAL HOMES, INC.
3408 EAST 11TH PLACE
BIG SPRING, TX 79720
MIKE BRIGNOLE
(915) 263-2300

SILVER CREEK HOMES
P.O. BOX 150
HWY. 148 SOUTH
HENRIETTA, TX 76365
DAVID SILVERTOOTH
(817) 538-6600

SOUTHERN ENERGY HOMES OF TEXAS
8701 HARMON ROAD
P.O. BOX 161157 (ZIP 76161)
FORT WORTH, TX 76179
GENERAL MANAGER
(817) 847-1355

VERMONT

SKYLINE CORP.
HIGHWAY 22A
FAIR HAVEN, VT 05743
GENERAL MANAGER
(802) 265-4954

VIRGINIA

COMMODORE CORP.
P.O. BOX 300
ROUTE 729
DANVILLE, VA 24541
GENERAL MANAGER
(804) 793-8811

FLEETWOOD HMS. OF VA #19-2
90 WEAVER ST.
ROCKY MOUNT, VA 24151
GARY CLARK
(540) 483-2929

FLEETWOOD HOMES OF VA #19
P.O. BOX 100
R.F.D. #4 HIGHWAY 40 W.
ROCKY MT., VA 24151
GENERAL MANAGER
(703) 483-5171

VIRGINIA HOMES, INC.
P.O. BOX 410
HIGHWAY 58 EAST
BOYDTON, VA 23917
GENERAL MANAGER
(804) 738-6107

WASHINGTON

FLEETWOOD HOMES OF WA #31
P.O. BOX 250
211-5TH STREET
WOODLAND, WA 98674
GENERAL MANAGER
(360) 225-9461

MODULINE INTERNATIONAL
P.O. BOX 1106
124 HABIEN ROAD
CHEHALIS, WA 98532
GENERAL MANAGER
(360) 748-8881

VALLEY MANUFACTURED
    HOUSING, INC.
1717 S. 4TH STREET
SUNNYSIDE, WA 98944
GENERAL MANAGER
(509) 839-9409

WISCONSIN

LIBERTY HOMES, INC.
P.O. BOX 228
DORCHESTER, WI 54425
GENERAL MANAGER
(715) 654-5021

LIBERTY/BADGER HOMES
P.O. BOX 110
#1 LIBERTY DRIVE
DORCHESTER, WI 54425
BEN FINLEY
(715) 654-5021

SKYLINE CORP./HOMETTE
P.O. BOX 590
HIGHWAY 61 NORTHEAST
LANCASTER, WI 53813
GENERAL MANAGER
(608) 723-4171

WICK BUILDING
SYSTEMS/MARSHFLD
P.O. BOX 530
2301 EAST 4TH STREET
MARSHFIELD, WI 54449
GENERAL MANAGER
(715) 387-2551

Appendix D

FTC REGIONAL OFFICES AND STATE CONSUMER PROTECTION OFFICES

D.1 FTC MAIN OFFICE

The FTC works for the consumer to prevent fraudulent, deceptive and unfair business practices in the marketplace and to provide information to help consumers spot, stop, and avoid them. To file a complaint, or to get free information on any of 150 consumer topics, call toll-free, 1-877-FTC-HELP (1-877-382-4357), or use the complaint form at www.ftc.gov. The FTC enters Internet, telemarketing, and other fraud-related complaints into Consumer Sentinel, a secure, online database available to hundreds of civil and criminal law enforcement agencies in the U.S and abroad.

Consumer Response Center
  Federal Trade Commission (FTC)
  600 Pennsylvania Avenue, NW
  Washington, DC 20580
  Toll free: 1-877-FTC-HELP (877-382-4357)
  TDD/TTY: 202-326-2502
  Web site: www.ftc.gov

D.2 FEDERAL TRADE COMMISSION (FTC) REGIONAL OFFICES

For information regarding filing a complaint with the FTC, contact the nearest regional office. The FTC has also developed resource guides to help consumers find the appropriate agencies to contact about consumer-related matters. These guides contain lists of nonprofit, state and local agencies for the states listed below.

The Northwest Region serves the residents of the following states: **Alaska, Idaho, Montana, Oregon, Washington** and **Wyoming**.

> Northwest Region
> Federal Trade Commission
> 2896 Federal Building, 915 Second Avenue
> Seattle, WA 98174

The Southeast Region serves the residents of the following states: **Alabama, Florida, Georgia, Mississippi, North Carolina, South Carolina,** and **Tennessee**.

> Southeast Region
> Federal Trade Commission
> Suite 1500
> 225 Peachtree Street., NE
> Atlanta, GA 30303

The Southwest Region serves the residents of the following states: **Arkansas, Louisiana, New Mexico, Oklahoma,** and **Texas**.

> Southwest Region
> Federal Trade Commission
> 1999 Bryan Street, Suite 2150
> Dallas, TX 75201-6808

The Western Region has **two** offices serving the residents of the following states: **Arizona**, **Northern California**, **Southern California**, **Colorado**, **Hawaii**, **Nevada** and **Utah**.

Western Region
Federal Trade Commission
901 Market Street, Suite 570
San Francisco, CA 94103

Western Region
Federal Trade Commission
10877 Wilshire Blvd., Suite 700
Los Angeles, California 90024

The Northeast Region serves the residents of the following states and/or territories: **Connecticut**, **Maine**, **Massachusetts**, **New Hampshire**, **New Jersey**, **New York**, **Puerto Rico**, **Rhode Island**, **Vermont**, and **U.S. Virgin Islands**.

Northeast Region
Federal Trade Commission
1 Bowling Green
New York, NY 10004

The East Central Region serves the residents of the following states: **Delaware**, **District of Columbia**, **Maryland**, **Michigan**, **Ohio**, **Pennsylvania**, **Virginia** and **West Virginia**.

East Central Region
Federal Trade Commission
1111 Superior Avenue, Suite 200
Cleveland, OH 44114-2507

The Midwest Region serves the residents of the following states: **Illinois, Indiana, Iowa, Kansas, Kentucky, Nebraska, North Dakota, Minnesota, Missouri, South Dakota**, and **Wisconsin**.

Midwest Region
Federal Trade Commission
55 East Monroe Street, Suite 1860
Chicago, IL 60603-5701

D.3 STATE ATTORNEY GENERAL AND OTHER STATE, COUNTY AND CITY GOVERNMENT CONSUMER PROTECTION OFFICES[1]

City, county and state consumer protection offices provide consumers with important services. They might mediate complaints, conduct investigations, prosecute offenders of consumer laws, license, and regulate a variety of professionals, promote strong consumer protection legislation, provide educational materials, and advocate in the consumer interest.

City and county consumer offices are familiar with local businesses and local ordinances and state laws. If there is no local consumer office in your area, contact your state consumer office. State offices, sometimes in a separate department of consumer affairs or the attorney general's or governor's office, are familiar with state laws and look for statewide patterns of problems. Consumer protection offices in the U.S. territories also are included.

To save time, call the office before sending in a written complaint. Ask if the office handles the type of complaint you have or if complaint forms are provided.

Many offices distribute consumer materials specifically geared to state laws and local issues. Call to obtain available educational information on your problem.

This list is arranged in alphabetical order by state name. State, county, and city jurisdictions and TDD numbers are in bold type.

---

[1] *Appendix C.3 is reprinted from the 2002 Consumer Action Handbook, published by the Consumer Information Center, U.S. General Services Administration. This list is also available on the Internet at www.pueblo.gsa.gov/chr.*

ALABAMA
State Offices
Ellen Leonard, Assistant Attorney General
Office of the Attorney General
Consumer Affairs Section
11 South Union Street
Montgomery, AL 36130
334-242-7335
Toll free in AL: 1-800-392-5658
Web site: www.ago.state.al.us

ALASKA
State Offices
Consumer Protection Unit
Office of the Attorney General
1031 West 4th Avenue
Suite 200
Anchorage, AK 99501-5903
907-269-5100
Fax: 907-276-8554
Web site: www.law.state.ak.us

ARIZONA
State Offices
Robert Zumoff, Chief Counsel
Consumer Protection and Advocacy Section
Office of the Attorney General
1275 West Washington Street
Phoenix, AZ 85007
602-542-3702
602-542-5763
    (consumer information and complaints)
Toll free in AZ: 1-800-352-8431
TDD: 602-542-5002
Fax: 602-542-4579
Web site: www.ag.state.az.us

Noreen Matts, Assistant Attorney General
Office of the Attorney General
Consumer Protection
400 West Congress South Bldg., Suite 315
Tucson, AZ 85701
520-628-6504
Toll free in AZ: 1-800-352-8431
Fax: 520-628-6532

County Offices
Derick Rapier, County Attorney
Greenlee County Attorney's Office
P.O. Box 1717
Clifton, AZ 85533
928-865-4108
Fax: 928-865-4665

Terence Hance, County Attorney
Coconino County Attorney's Office
110 East Chernue Avenue
Flagstaff, AZ 86001
928-779-6518
Fax: 928-779-5618

Robert Olson, Pinal County Attorney
Pinal County Attorney's Office
P.O. Box 887
Florence, AZ 85232
520-868-6271
Fax: 520-868-6521

James W. Hazel Jr., County Attorney
Gila County Attorney's Office
1400 East Ash Street
Globe, AZ 85501
928-425-3231 ext. 298
Fax: 928-425-3720

Melvin Bowers, County Attorney
Navajo County Attorney's Office
P.O. Box 668
Holbrook, AZ 86025
928-524-4026
Fax: 928-524-4244

William Ekstrom, County Attorney
Mohave County Attorney's Office
315 North 4th Street
P.O. Box 7000
Kingman, AZ 86402-7000
928-753-0719
Fax: 928-753-2669

Martha Chase, County Attorney
Santa Cruz County Attorney's Office
2150 North Congress Dr., Ste. 201
Nogales, AZ 85621
520-375-7780
Fax: 520-761-7859

County Attorney
1320 Kofa Avenue
P.O. Box 709
Parker, AZ 85344
928-669-6118
Fax: 928-669-2019

Shelia Sullivan Polk, County Attorney
Yavapai County Attorney's Office
Yavapai County Courthouse
255 East Gurley
Prescott, AZ 86301
520-771-3344
Fax: 520-771-3110

Graham County Attorney's Office
Graham County Courthouse
800 West Main
Safford, AZ 85546
928-428-3620
Fax: 928-428-7200

Apache County Attorney's Office
P.O. Box 637
St. Johns, AZ 85936
928-337-4364, ext. 240
Fax: 928-337-2427

Patricia A. Orozco, County Attorney
Yuma County Attorney's Office
168 South Second Avenue
Yuma, AZ 85364
928-329-2270
Fax: 928-329-2284

City Offices
L. Michael Anderson, Deputy City Attorney
Consumer Affairs Division
Tucson City Attorney's Office
1501 N. Oracle Annex
P.O. Box 27210
Tucson, AZ 85705
520-791-4886
Fax: 520-791-4991

ARKANSAS
State Offices
Consumer Protection Division
Office of the Attorney General
323 Center Street
Suite 200
Little Rock, AR 72201
501-682-2007
501-682-2341 Consumer Hotline
1-800-448-3014 Crime Victims Hotline
501-682-1334 Local Do Not Call Program
1-877-866-8225 In State Do Not Call Program
Toll free: 1-800-482-8982
TDD: 501-682-6073
Fax: 501-682-8118
E-mail: consumer@ag.state.ar.us
Web site: www.ag.state.ar.us

BERMUDA
Offices
Department of Consumer Affairs
Ingham and Wilkinson Building
129 Front Street
Hamilton, Bermuda, BE HM 12
441-297-7627
Fax: 441-295-6892
E-mail: mcsharpe@bdagov@bm

CALIFORNIA
State Offices
Bill Lockyer, Attorney General
Office of the Attorney General
Public Inquiry Unit
P.O. Box 944255
Sacramento, CA 94244-2550
916-322-3360
Toll free in CA: 1-800-952-5225
TDD: 916-324-5564
Web site: www.caag.state.ca.us/pi

Bureau of Automotive Repair
California Department of Consumer Affairs
Sacramento, CA 95827
916-255-4565
Toll free in CA: 1-800-952-5210
TDD: 916-255-1369
Web site: www.smogcheck.ca.gov

California Department of Consumer Affairs
400 R Street
Suite 3000
Sacramento, CA 95814
916-445-4465
916-445-2643
(Correspondence and Complaint Review Unit)
Toll free in CA: 1-800-952-5210
TDD/TTY: 916-322-1700
or **1-800-326-2297**
Web site: www.dca.ca.gov

County Offices
Michael Yraceburn, Supervising Deputy
   District Attorney
Criminal Division
Kern County District Attorney's Office
1215 Truxtun Avenue
4th Floor
Bakersfield, CA 93301
661-868-2350
Fax: 661-868-2135
E-mail: ymichael@co.kern.ca.us

Criselda Gonzalez, Deputy District Attorney
Consumer Affairs Unit
Solano County District Attorney's Office
600 Union Avenue
Fairfield, CA 94533
707-421-6859
707-421-6800
Fax: 707-421-7986

Alan Yengoyan, Senior Deputy District Attorney
Business Affairs Unit
Fresno County District Attorney's Office
1250 Van Ness Avenue
2nd Floor
Fresno, CA 93721
559-488-3836
559-488-3156
Fax: 559-485-1315

Pastor Herrera, Jr., Director
Los Angeles County Department of
Consumer Affairs
500 West Temple Street
Room B-96
Los Angeles, CA 90012-2706
213-974-1452
Fax: 213-687-0233
Web site: consumer-affairs.co.la.ca.us

James L. Sepulveda, Sr. Deputy District Attorney
Contra Costa County District Attorney's
Office
651 Pine Street, 12th floor
Martinez, CA 94553
925-646-4620
Fax: 925-646-4683

Consumer Fraud Unit
Stanislaus County District Attorney's Office
P.O. Box 442
Modesto, CA 95353-0442
209-525-5550
Fax: 209-525-5545
Web site: www.stanislaus-da.org

Gary Lieberstien, Deputy District Attorney
Consumer Affairs Division
Napa County District Attorney's Office
931 Parkway Mall
P.O. Box 720
Napa, CA 94559
707-253-4211
707-253-4059
Fax: 707-253-4041

John Wilson, Deputy in Charge
Consumer & Environmental Unit
San Mateo County District Attorney's Office
400 County Center
4th Floor
Redwood City, CA 94063
650-363-4651

M. Scott Prentice, Supervising Deputy District
Attorney
Consumer and Environmental Protection
Division
Sacramento County District Attorney's Office
P.O. Box 749
906 G Street, Ste. 700
Sacramento, CA 95812-0749
916-874-6174
Fax: 916-874-7660

Consumer Protection Division
P.O. Box 1131
Salinas, CA 93902
831-755-5073
Fax: 831-755-5608

Gregg McClain, Supervising Duputy District
Attorney
San Diego County District Attorney's Office
P.O. Box 121011
San Diego, CA 92112-1011
619-531-4070
Fax: 619-531-4481

San Francisco County District Attorney's Office
732 Brannan Street, #322
San Francisco, CA 94103
415-551-9595 (public inquiries)

Al Bender, Supervising Deputy District Attorney
Santa Clara County District Attorney's
Consumer Protection Unit
70 West Hedding Street
West Wing, 4th Floor
San Jose, CA 95110
408-792-2880 (consumer protection)
408-792-2881 (small claims advisory)
Fax: 408-279-8742
Web site: www.santaclara-
da.org/consumer.html

Consumer Protection Division
Marin County District Attorney's Office
3501 Civic Center Drive
San Rafael, CA 94903
415-499-6450
Fax: 415-499-3719
E-mail: consumer@marin.org
Web site: www.marin.org/mc/da

Barbara Kob, Mediation Coordinator
Marin County Mediation Services
4 Jeannette Prandi Way
San Rafael, CA 94903
415-499-7454
Fax: 415-499-6978

Consumer/Environmental Protection Unit
Orange County District Attorney's Office
405 West 5th Street, Suite 606
Santa Ana, CA 92701
714-834-3600

Allan Kaplan, Senior Deputy District Attorney
Consumer Protection Unit
Santa Barbara County District Attorney's Office
1105 Santa Barbara Street
Santa Barbara, CA 93101
805-568-2300
Fax: 805-568-2398

Robin Gysin, Coordinator
Division of Consumer Affairs
Santa Cruz County District Attorney's Office
701 Ocean Street
Room 200
Santa Cruz, CA 95060
831-454-2050
TDD/TTY: 831-454-2123
Fax: 831-454-2920
E-mail: dat155@co.santa-cruz.ca.us
Web site: www.CO.Santa-Cruz.CA/US

Franklin Stephenson, Supervising Deputy
   District Attorney
San Joaquin County District Attorney's Office
Consumer Affairs Prosecution Unit
222 East Weber, Room 412
P.O. Box 990
Stockton, CA 95202
209-468-9321
Fax: 209-468-0314

Norman L. Vroman, District Attorney
Mendocino County District Attorney's Office
P.O. Box 1000
Ukiah, CA 95482
707-463-4211
Fax: 707-463-4687

Melodianne Duffy, Supervisor
Consumer Mediation Section
Ventura County District Attorney's Office
800 South Victoria Avenue
Ventura, CA 93009
805-654-3110
Fax: 805-648-9255
Web site: www.ventura.org/vcda

Consumer Fraud and Environmental
   Prosecution Unit
Tulare County District Attorney's Office
Visalia, CA 93291
559-733-6411
Fax: 559-730-2658

City Offices
Donald Kass, Supervising Deputy City Attorney
Consumer Protection Division
Los Angeles City Attorney's Office
200 North Main Street
1600 City Hall East
Los Angeles, CA 90012
213-485-4515
Fax: 213-847-0402
E-mail: dkass@atty.lacity.org

Michael D. Rivo, Head Deputy City Attorney
Consumer and Environmental Protection Unit
San Diego City Attorney's Office
1200 Third Avenue
Suite 700
San Diego, CA 92101-4106
619-533-5600
Web site: www.sannet.gov/city-attorney

Adam Radinsky, Deputy City Attorney
Consumer Protection and Fair Housing
1685 Main Street
Room 310
Santa Monica, CA 90401
310-458-8336
Fax: 310-395-6727
E-mail: consumers@ci.santa-monica.ca.us
Web site: pen.ci.santa-monica.ca.us/atty/
   consumer_protection/

COLORADO
State Offices
Consumer Protection Division
Colorado Attorney General's Office
5th Floor
Denver, CO 80203-1760
303-866-5189
303-866-5125
Toll free: 1-800-332-2071
Fax: 303-866-5443

County Offices
David Zook, Chief Deputy District Attorney
Economic Crime Division
El Paso and Teller Counties District Attorney's
    Office
105 East Vermijo, Suite 205
Colorado Springs, CO 80903-2083
719-520-6002
Fax: 719-520-6006
E-mail: david_zook@co.el-paso.co.us
Web site: www.co.el-paso.co.us/
    districtattorney/scam.htm

Phillip Parrott, Chief Deputy District Attorney
Denver District Attorney's Economic Crimes
    Unit
303 West Colfax Ave., Ste. 1300
Denver, CO 80204
720-913-9179
TDD/TTY: 720-913-9182
Fax: 720-913-9177
Web site: www.denverda.org

Sarah Law, District Attorney
Archuleta, LaPlata and San Juan Counties
District Attorney's Office
P.O. Drawer 3455
Durango, CO 81302
970-247-8850
Fax: 970-259-0200

Weld County District Attorney's Office
P.O. Box 1167
Greeley, CO 80632
970-356-4010
Fax: 970-352-8023

Gus Sandstrom, District Attorney
Pueblo County District Attorney's Office
201 West 8th Street, Suite 801
Pueblo, CO 81003
719-583-6030
Fax: 719-583-6666

CONNECTICUT
State Offices
Philip Rosario, Assistant Attorney General
Consumer Protection
Office of Attorney General
110 Sherman Street
Hartford, CT 06105
860-808-5400
Fax: 860-808-5585
Web site: www.cslnet.ctstateu.edu/attygenl

Department of Consumer Protection
165 Capitol Avenue
Hartford, CT 06106
860-713-6300
Toll free in CT: 1-800-842-2649
Fax: 860-566-1531
Web site: www.state.ct.us/dcp/

City Offices
City of Middletown
245 DeKoven Drive
P.O. Box 1300
Middletown, CT 06457-1300
860-344-3491
TDD: 860-344-3521
Fax: 860-344-3561
E-mail: phil.cacciola@cityofmiddleton.com

DELAWARE
State Offices
Eugene M. Hall, Director
Fraud and Consumer Protection Division
Office of the Attorney General
820 North French Street
5th Floor
Wilmington, DE 19801
302-577-8600
Toll free in DE: 1-800-220-5424
Fax: 302-577-6987
Web site: www.state.de.us/attgen/consumer.htm

Consumer Protection Unit
Office of Attorney General
5th Floor
Wilmington, DE 19801
302-577-8600
Toll free in DE: 1-800-220-5424
Fax: 302-577-3090
Web site: www.state.de.us/attgen/consumer.htm

DISTRICT OF COLUMBIA
Offices
Bennett Rushkoff, Senior Counsel
Office of the Corporation Counsel
441 4th Street, NW
Suite 450-N
Washington, DC 20001
202-442-9828 (consumer hotline)
Fax: 202-727-6546

FLORIDA
State Offices
Cecile Dykas, Assistant Deputy Attorney
   General
Economic Crimes Division
Office of the Attorney General
110 SE 6th Street
Republic Tower, 10th Floor
Fort Lauderdale, FL 33301
954-712-4600
Fax: 954-712-4904
Web site: www.legal.firn.edu

Jack Norris, Chief of Multi-State Litigation
Consumer Litigation Section
110 SE 6th Street
Fort Lauderdale, FL 33301
954-712-4600
Fax: 954-712-4706

Economic Crimes Division
Office of the Attorney General
Century Plaza, Suite 1000
Orlando, FL 32801
407-999-5588
Fax: 407-245-0365

Les Garringer, Assistant Deputy Attorney
   General
Economic Crimes Division
Office of the Attorney General
The Capitol, Suite PL01
Tallahassee, FL 32399-1050
850-414-3300
Fax: 850-488-4483

James Kelly, Director of Division Consumer
   Services
Department of Agriculture & Consumer
   Services
407 South Calhoun Street
Mayo Building, 2nd Floor
Tallahassee, FL 32399-0800
850-922-2966
Toll free in FL: 1-800-435-7352
Fax: 850-487-4177
Web site: www.fl-ag.com

County Offices
Sheryl Lord, Director
Pinellas County Office of Consumer Protection
15251 Roosevelt Blvd
Suite 209
Clearwater, FL 33760
727-464-6200
TDD/TTY: 727-464-6088
Fax: 727-464-6129
Web site: www.co.pinellas.fl.us/bcc

Broward County Consumer Affairs Division
115 South Andrews Avenue
Annex Room A460
Fort Lauderdale, FL 33301
954-765-5350, ext. 232
Fax: 954-765-5309
E-mail: mfandel@co.broward.fl.us
Web site: www.co.broward.fl.us

Frederic Kerstein, Chief
Dade County Economic Crime Unit
Office of the State Attorney
1350 NW 12th Avenue
5th Floor, Graham Building
Miami, FL 33136-2111
305-547-0671
Fax: 305-547-0717
E-mail: kerstef@sa11.state.fl.us

Sheila Rushton, Director
Consumer Services Department
Miami-Dade County
140 West Flagler Street
Suite 903
Miami, FL 33130
305-375-3677 (Consumer Hotline)
TDD/TTY: 305-375-4177
Fax: 305-375-4120
E-mail: consumer@miamidade.gov
Web site: www.co.miami-dade.fl.us/csd

Carol A. McCarthy, Investigator
Pasco County Consumer Affairs Division
7530 Little Road
New Port Richey, FL 34654
727-847-8106
352-521-5179
Fax: 727-847-8191

Carlos J. Morales, Chief Investigator
Orange County Consumer Fraud Unit
415 North Orange Avenue
P.O. Box 1673
Orlando, FL 32802
407-836-2490
Fax: 407-836-2376
E-mail: fraudhelp@sao9.org
Web site: www.onetgov.net

Hillsborough County Consumer Protection
   Agency
8900 N. Armenia Ave., Ste. 222
Tampa, FL 33604-1067
813-903-3430
Fax: 813-903-3432
Web site: www.hillsboroughcounty.org

Dennis Moore, Director
Palm Beach County Division of Consumer
   Affairs
50 South Military Trail, Suite 201
West Palm Beach, FL 33415
561-233-4820
Toll free: 1-800-930-5124 (Palm Beach County)
Fax: 561-233-4838
E-mail: consumer@co.palm-beach.fl.us

City Offices
Sandra Hull-Richardson, Chief of Consumer
   Affairs
City of Jacksonville Division of Consumer
   Affairs
St. James Building
117 West Duval Street, Suite M-100
Jacksonville, FL 32202
904-630-3467
Fax: 904-630-3458
Web site: www.coj.net/pub/consumer/
   consumer.ht

Economic Crimes Division
Office of the Attorney General
2002 North Lois Ave, Suite 520
Tampa, FL 33607
813-801-0600
Fax: 813-871-7262

GEORGIA
State Offices
Barry Reid, Administrator
Governor's Office of Consumer Affairs
2 Martin Luther King, Jr. Drive
Suite 356
Atlanta, GA 30334
404-656-3790
Toll free in GA (outside Atlanta area):
   1-800-869-1123
Fax: 404-651-9018
Web site: www2.state.ga.us/gaoca

HAWAII
State Offices
Gene Murayama, Investigator
Office of Consumer Protection
Department of Commerce and Consumer
   Affairs
345 Kekuanaoa Street, Room 12
Hilo, HI 96720
808-933-0910
Fax: 808-933-8845

Stephen Levins, Acting Executive Director
Office of Consumer Protection
Department of Commerce and Consumer
   Affairs
235 South Beretania Street
Room 801
Honolulu, HI 96813
808-586-2636
Fax: 808-586-2640

Office of Consumer Protection
Dept of Commerce and Consumer Affairs
Wailuku, HI 96793
808-984-8244
Fax: 808-243-5807
Web site: www.state.hi.us/dcca/

IDAHO
State Offices
Consumer Protection Unit
Idaho Attorney General's Office
Boise, ID 83720-0010
208-334-2424
Toll free in ID: 1-800-432-3545
Fax: 208-334-2830
Web site: www.state.id.us/ag

ILLINOIS
State Offices
Office of the Attorney General
1001 East Main Street
Carbondale, IL 62901
618-529-6400
Toll free in IL: 1-800-243-0607
(consumer hotline serving southern Illinois)
TDD: 618-529-0607
Fax: 618-529-6416

Charles Fergus, Bureau Chief
Consumer Fraud Bureau
100 West Randolph
12th Floor
Chicago, IL 60601
312-814-3580
Toll free in IL: 1-800-386-5438
TDD: 312-814-3374
Fax: 312-814-2549 or 312-814-3806
Web site: www.ag.state.il.us

Patricia Kelly, Chief
Consumer Protection Division of the Attorney
General Office
100 West Randolph
12th Floor
Chicago, IL 60601
312-814-3000
TDD: 312-793-2852
Fax: 312-814-2593

Governor's Office of Citizens Assistance
222 South College, Room 106
Springfield, IL 62706
217-782-0244
Toll free in IL: 1-800-642-3112
Fax: 217-524-4049
E-mail: governor@state.il.us

County Offices
Cook County State Attorney's Office
Consumer Fraud Division
69 West Washington
Suite 700
Chicago, IL 60091
312-603-8700

William Haine, State's Attorney
Madison County Office of State's Attorney
157 North Main Street, Suite 402
Edwardsville, IL 62025
618-692-6280
Fax: 618-656-7312

Department of Consumer Affairs serving
Central Illinois
Office of the Attorney General
Springfield, IL 62706
217-782-1090
Toll free in IL: 1-800-243-0618
217-785-2771
Fax: 217-782-1097
E-mail: agconsmr@mail.state.il.us
Web site: www.ag.state.il.us

City Offices
Caroline Shoenberger, Commissioner
Chicago Department of Consumer Services
121 North LaSalle Street
Room 808
Chicago, IL 60602
312-744-4006
TDD: 312-744-9385
Fax: 312-744-9089
Web site: www.ci.chi.il.us/ConsumerServices/

INDIANA
State Offices
Consumer Protection Division
Office of the Attorney General
402 West Washington Street, 5th Floor
Indianapolis, IN 46204
317-232-6201
Toll free in IN: 1-800-382-5516
Consumer Hotline
Fax: 317-232-7979
Web site: www.in.gov/attorneygeneral

County Offices
Marrion County Prosecuting Attorney's Office
560 City-County Building
200 East Washington Street
Indianapolis, IN 46204-3363
317-327-3892
TDD/TTY: 317-327-5186
Fax: 317-327-5409
Web site: www.indygov.org

IOWA
State Offices
William Brauch, Assistant Attorney General
Consumer Protection Division
Office of the Attorney General
Director of Consumer Protection Division
1300 East Walnut Street, 2nd Floor
Des Moines, IA 50319
515-281-5926
Fax: 515-281-6771
E-mail: consumer@ag.state.ia.us
Web site: www.IowaAttorneyGeneral.org

KANSAS
State Offices
Consumer Protection Division
Office of the Attorney General
4th Floor
Topeka, KS 66612-1597
785-296-3751
Toll free in KS: 1-800-432-2310
TDD/TTY: 785-291-3767
Fax: 785-291-3699
E-mail: cprotect@ksag.org
Web site: www.ink.org/public/ksag

Office of the District Attorney
Consumer Fraud & Economic Crime Division
Wichita, KS 67203-3747
316-383-7921
Toll free in KS: 1-800-432-2310
Fax: 316-383-4669

County Offices
Johnson County District Attorney's Office
Consumer Protection Division
Johnson County Courthouse
100 North Kansas Ave.
Olathe, KS 66061
913-715-3003
Fax: 913-715-3040

KENTUCKY
State Offices
Consumer Protection Division
Office of the Attorney General
1024 Capital Center Drive
Frankfort, KY 40601
502-696-5389
Toll free in KY: 1-888-432-9257
Fax: 502-573-8317
E-mail: consumerprotection@law.state.ky.us
Web site: www.kyattorneygeneral.com/cp

Harold Turner, Assistant Attorney General
Consumer Protection Division
Office of the Attorney General
9001 Shelbyville Road
Suite 3
Louisville, KY 40222
502-425-4825
Fax: 502-573-8317 Lori

LOUISIANA
State Offices
Isabel Wingerter, Chief
Consumer Protection Section
Office of the Attorney General
301 Main Street, Suite 1250
Baton Rouge, LA 70801
Toll free nationwide: 1-800-351-4889
Fax: 225-342-9637
Web site: www.ag.state.la.us

County Offices
Andrea Ragas
Consumer Protection Section
Jefferson Parish District Attorney
200 Derbigny Street
5th Floor Courthouse Annex
Gretna, LA 70053
504-368-1020
Fax: 504-368-4562

MAINE
State Offices
Maine Attorney General's Consumer
Mediation Service
6 State House Station
Augusta, ME 04333
207-626-8800
Web site: www.state.me.us/ag

Public Protection Division
Office of the Attorney General
Augusta, ME 04333
207-626-8849

William Lund, Director
Office of Consumer Credit Regulation
35 State House Station
Augusta, ME 04333-0035
207-624-8527
Toll free in ME: 1-800-332-8529
TDD/TTY: 207-624-8563
Fax: 207-582-7699
Web site: www.mainecreditreg.org

MARYLAND
State Offices
Consumer Protection Division
Office of the Attorney General
16th Floor
Baltimore, MD 21202-2021
410-528-8662 (consumer complaint hotline)
410-576-6550 (consumer information)
TDD: 410-576-6372 (Maryland only)
Fax: 410-576-7040
E-mail: consumer@oag.state.md.us
Web site: www.oag.state.md.us/consumer

Business Licensing & Consumer Service
Motor Vehicle Administration
Glen Burnie, MD 21062
410-768-7248
Fax: 410-768-7602

Regional Offices
Larry Munson, Administrator
Maryland Attorney Generals' Office
Consumer Protection Division
138 East Antietam St, Ste. 210
Hagerstown, MD 21740-5684
301-791-4780
410-576-6372
Fax: 301-791-7178

Eastern Shore Branch Office
Consumer Protection Division
Office of the Attorney General
201 Baptist Street
Suite 30
Salisbury, MD 21801-4976
410-543-6620
Fax: 410-543-6642
Web site: www.oag.state.md.us

County Offices
Stephen Hannan, Administrator
Howard County Office of Consumer Affairs
6751 Columbia Gateway Drive
Columbia, MD 21046
410-313-6420
Fax: 410-313-6453
E-mail: shannan@co.ho.md.us

Montgomery County Division of Consumer
   Affairs
100 Maryland Avenue
Suite 330
Rockville, MD 20850
240-777-3636
TDD: 240-777-3679
Fax: 240-777-3768
Web site: www.co.mo.md.us/hca

MASSACHUSETTS
State Offices
Tom Reilly, Attorney General
Consumer Protection and Antitrust Division
Office of the Attorney General
200 Portland Street
Boston, MA 02114
617-727-8400 The Consumer Hotline —
   information and referral to local county
   and city government consumer offices
   (listed below) that work in conjunction with
   the Department of the Attorney General
Fax: 617-727-3265
Web site: www.ago.state.ma.us

Jennifer Davis Carey, Director
Executive Office of Consumer Affairs and
  Business Regulation
10 Park Plaza, Room 5170
Boston, MA 02116
617-973-8700 general info
617-973-8787 consumer hotline
in MA 1-888-283-3757
TDD/TTY: 617-973-8790
Fax: 617-973-8798
E-mail: consumer@state.ma.us
Web site: www.state.ma.us/consumer

Consumer Protection and Antitrust Division
Office of the Attorney General — Springfield
436 Dwight Street
Springfield, MA 01103
413-784-1240
Fax: 413-784-1244

County Offices
Mayor's Office of Consumer Affairs and
  Licensing
Boston City Hall
Room 817
Boston, MA 02201
617-635-3834
617-635-4165
Fax: 617-635-4174

Cambridge Consumers' Council
831 Massachusetts Ave
Cambridge, MA 02139
617-349-6150
Fax: 617-349-6148
Web site: www.ci.cambridge.ma.us/~Consumer

Fall River Consumer Program
One Government Center
Fall River, MA 02722
508-324-2672
Fax: 508-324-2626

Consumer Protection Division
North Western District Attorney's Office
238 Main Street
Greenfield, MA 01301
413-774-5102
Fax: 413-773-3278

Consumer Protection Program
Haverhill Community Action, Inc.
25 Locust Street
Haverhill, MA 01830
978-373-1971
Fax: 978-373-8966

Consumer Assistance Council, Inc.
149 Main Street
Hyannis, MA 02601
508-771-0700
Toll free: 1-800-867-0701
Fax: 508-771-3011
Web site: www.consumercouncil.com

Greater Lawrence Community Action Council,
  Inc.
Consumer Protection Program
Lawrence, MA 08140
978-681-4990
Fax: 978-681-4949
Web site: www.glcac.org

Middlesex Community College Law Center
Local Consumer Program
33 Kearney Square, Room 117
Lowell, MA 01852
978-656-3342
Fax: 978-656-3339
E-mail: dunnk@middlesex.cc.ma.us

Consumer Assistance Office — Metro West, Inc.
209 West Central Street
Natick, MA 01760
508-651-8812
Fax: 508-647-0661

Newton-Brookline Consumer Office
Newton City Hall
1000 Commonwealth Ave.
Newton, MA 02465
617-552-7205
Fax: 617-552-7027

Mass PIRG Consumer Action Center
182 Green Street
North Weymouth, MA 02191
781-335-0280
Fax: 781-340-3991
E-mail: jfoyconsumeraction2@juno.com

Berkshire County Consumer Advocates, Inc.
150 North Street
Pittsfield, MA 01201
413-443-9128
Toll free: 1-800-540-9128
Fax: 413-496-9225

South Shore Community Action Council, Inc.
265 South Meadow Road
Plymouth, MA 02360
508-747-7575 x226
Fax: 508-746-5140
E-mail: lmtilley@sscac.org

Mayor's Office of Consumer Information
City of Springfield
1243 Main St.
Springfield, MA 01103
413-787-6437

Consumer Council of Worcester County
484 Main Street
2nd Floor
Worcester, MA 01608-1690
508-754-1176
Fax: 508-754-0203
E-mail: dreilly@wcac.net

MICHIGAN
State Offices
Stanley F. Pruss, Assistant in Charge
Consumer Protection Division
Office of Attorney General
P.O. Box 30213
Lansing, MI 48909
517-373-1140 (complaint information)
517-373-1110
Fax: 517-241-3771

Rodger James, Director
Bureau of Automotive Regulation
Michigan Department of State
Lansing, MI 48918-1200
517-373-4777
Toll free in MI: 1-800-292-4204
Fax: 517-373-0964

County Offices
Mike Studders, Chief Investigator
Bay County Consumer Protection Unit
1230 Washington - Courthouse
Bay City, MI 48707-5994
517-895-4139
Fax: 517-895-4167

Margaret DeMuynck, Director
Consumer Protection Department
Macomb County
Office of the Prosecuting Attorney
Macomb County Administration Bldg
One South Main Street, 3rd FL
Mt. Clemens, MI 48043
810-469-5600
810-469-5350
Fax: 810-469-5609

City Offices
John Roy Castillo, J.D., Director
City of Detroit Consumer Affairs Department
65 Cadillac Square
Suite 1600
Detroit, MI 48226
313-224-3508
313-224-6995 (complaints)
Fax: 313-224-2796
E-mail: castillojr@cadtwr.ci.detroit.mi.us
Web site: www.ci.detroit.mi.us

MINNESOTA
State Offices
Charles Ferguson, Manager
Consumer Services Division
Minnesota Attorney General's Office
1400 NCL Tower
445 Minnesota Street
St. Paul, MN 55101
612-296-3353
Toll free: 1-800-657-3787
Fax: 612-282-5801
E-mail: consumer.ag@state.mn.us
Web site: www.ag.state.mn.us/consumer

County Offices
Roshan Rajkumar, Director, Citizens Info
  Hotline
Hennepin County Citizen Information Hotline
  Office of Hennepin County Attorney
  C-2000 County Government Center
Minneapolis, MN 55487
612-348-4528
TDD/TTY: 612-348-6015
Fax: 612-348-9712
E-mail: citizeninfo@hennipin.mn.us
Web site:
  www.co.hennepin.mn.us/coatty/hcatty.htm

City Offices
James Moncur, Director
Division of Licenses & Consumer Services
Minneapolis Department of Regulatory Services
City Hall, Room 1C
350 South 5th Street
Minneapolis, MN 55415
612-673-2080
TDD/TTY: 612-673-3300/3360
Fax: 612-673-3399
E-mail: opa@ci.minneapolis.mn.us
Web site: www.ci.minneapolis.mn.us

MISSISSIPPI
State Offices
Julie McLemoil, Director
Bureau of Regulatory Services
Department of Agriculture and Commerce
121 North Jefferson Street
P.O. Box 1609
Jackson, MS 39201
601-359-1111
Fax: 601-354-6502
Web site: www.mdac.state.ms.us

Michael D. Rhodes, Director
Consumer Protection Division of the
 Mississippi Attorney General's Office
P.O. Box 22947
Jackson, MS 39225-2947
601-359-4230
Toll free in MS: 1-800-281-4418
Fax: 601-359-4231
Web site: www.ago.state.ms.us

MISSOURI
State Offices
William J. Bryan, Deputy Chief Counsel
Consumer Protection and Trade Offense
 Division
P.O. Box 899
1530 Rax Court
Jefferson City, MO 65102
573-751-6887
573-751-3321
Toll free in MO: 1-800-392-8222
TDD/TTY toll free in MO: 1-800-729-8668
Fax: 573-751-7948
E-mail: attgenmail@moago.org
Web site: www.ago.state.mo.us

MONTANA
State Offices
Consumer Affairs Unit
Department of Administration
Box 200501
Helena, MT 59620-0501
406-444-4312 (Misc.)
406-444-9405 (Telemarketing)
406-444-1588 (Automotive)
Fax: 406-444-2903

NEBRASKA
State Offices
Jason W Hayes, Assistant Attorney General
Department of Justice
2115 State Capitol
P.O. Box 98920
Lincoln, NE 68509
402-471-2682
Toll free in state: 1-800-727-6432
Fax: 402-471-0006
Web site: www.nol.org/homelago

NEVADA
State Offices
Bureau of Consumer Protection
555 E. Washington Ave, Ste. 3900
Las Vegas, NV 89101
702-486-3420

Patricia Jarman-Manning, Commissioner
Nevada Consumer Affairs Division
1850 East Sahara
Suite 101
Las Vegas, NV 89104
702-486-7355
Toll free: 1-800-326-5202
TDD: 702-486-7901
Fax: 702-486-7371
E-mail: ncad@fyiconsumer.org
Web site: www.fyiconsumer.org

Michael Hastings, Deputy Chief Investigator
Consumer Affairs Division
Department of Business and Industry
4600 Kietzke Lane, Building B, Suite 113
Reno, NV 89502
775-688-1800
Toll free in NV: 1-800-326-5202
TDD: 775-486-7901
Fax: 702-688-1803

NEW HAMPSHIRE
State Offices
Consumer Protection and Antitrust Bureau
New Hampshire Attorney General's Office
33 Capitol Street
Concord, NH 03301
603-271-3641
TDD toll free: 1-800-735-2964
Fax: 603-271-2110
Web site:
   www.state.nh.us/nhdoj/Consumer/cpb.html

NEW JERSEY
State Offices
Department of Law and Public Safety
New Jersey Division of Consumer Affairs
P.O. Box 45025
Newark, NJ 07101
973-504-6200
Toll free in NJ: 1-800-242-5846
Fax: 973-648-3538
E-mail: askconsumeraffairs@smtp.lps.state.nj.us
Web site: www.state.nj.us/lps/ca/home.htm

New Jersey Division of Law
P.O. Box 45029
124 Halsey Street, 5th Floor
Newark, NJ 07101
973-648-3453
Fax: 201-648-3879
E-mail: jacobcar@law.dol.lps.sate.nj.us

County Offices
William Ross III, Director
Atlantic County Division of Consumer Affairs
1333 Atlantic Avenue
8th Floor
Atlantic City, NJ 08401
609-343-2376
609-345-6700
Fax: 609-343-2322
Web site: www.aclink.org/conshome.htm

Camden County Office of Consumer
Protection/Weights and Measures
Jefferson House
Lakeland Road
Blackwood, NJ 08012
609-374-6161
609-374-6001
Toll free in NJ: 800-999-9045
Fax: 609-232-0748
E-mail: consumer@co.camden.nj.us
Web site: www.co.camden.nj.us

Department of Consumer Affairs & Weight
   & Measures
Cumberland County Department of Consumer
Affairs and Weights and Measures
Bridgeton, NJ 08302
856-453-2203
Fax: 856-453-2206
E-mail: louismo@co.cumberland.nj.us

Michael P. Brogan, Director/Superintendent
   Cape May County Consumer Affairs
   Weights and Measures
4 Moore Road
Cape May Court House, NJ 08210
609-463-6475
Fax: 609-465-4639
E-mail: mbrogan@co.cape-may.nj.us

Essex County Division of Consumer
Action/Consumer Services
50 South Clinton Street
Suite 3201
East Orange, NJ 07018
973-395-8350
Fax: 973-395-8433

Monmouth County Department of Consumer
   Affairs
50 East Main Street
P.O. Box 1255
Freehold, NJ 07728-1255
732-431-7900
Fax: 732-845-2037

John Wassberg, Director
Bergen County Office of Consumer Protection
21 Main Street
Room 101-E
Hackensack, NJ 07601-7000
201-646-2650
Fax: 201-489-6095

Willie L. Flood, Director
Hudson County Division of Consumer Affairs
595 Newark Avenue
Jersey City, NJ 07306
201-795-6295
201-795-6163
Fax: 201-795-6462

Hunterdon County Consumer Affairs
P.O. Box 283
Lebanon, NJ 08833
908-806-5174

Renee Borstad, Director/Superintendent
Burlington County Office of Consumer
Affairs/Weights and Measures
49 Rancocas Road
P.O. Box 6000
Mount Holly, NJ 08060
609-265-5098 Weights and Measures
609-265-5054 Consumer Affairs
Fax: 609-265-5065

Eileen Popovich, Director
Division of Consumer Affairs
Somerset County
P.O. Box 3000
Somerville, NJ 08876-1262
908-231-7000, ext. 7400
Fax: 908-429-0670
E-mail: consumeraffairs@co.somerset.nj.us
Web site: www.co.somerset.nj.us

Kenneth J. Leake, Director
Ocean County Department of Consumer
Affairs/Weights and Measures
1027 Hooper Avenue
P.O. Box 2191
Toms River, NJ 08754-2191
732-929-2105
Toll free in NJ: 1-800-722-0291 ex. 2105
Fax: 732-506-5330

Donna Giovannetti, Division Chief
Mercer County Consumer Affairs
640 South Broad St., Room 404
P.O. Box 8068
Trenton, NJ 08650-0068
609-989-6671
Fax: 609-989-6670

Ernest Salerno, Superintendent
Passaic County Department of Consumer
  Affairs
1310 Route 23 North
Wayne, NJ 07470
973-305-5881
Fax: 973-628-1796

Ernest N. Salerno, Superintendent
County of Passaic
Dept of Law and Public Safety
Div of Weights and Measures — CS
1310 Route 23 North
Wayne, NJ 07470
973-305-5750 (Wts & Meas)
973-305-5881 (Consumer Prot'n)
Fax: 973-628-1796
E-mail: pcca@advanix.net

Florence Peterson, Director
Union County Division of Consumer Affairs
300 North Avenue East
P.O. Box 186
Westfield, NJ 07091
908-654-9840
Fax: 908-654-3082
E-mail: fpeterson@unioncountynj.org
Web site: www.unioncountynj.org

Gloucester County Department of Consumer
Protection/Weights and Measures
152 North Broad Street
P.O. Box 337
Woodbury, NJ 08096
856-853-3349
856-853-3350
TDD: 856-848-6616
Fax: 609-853-6813
E-mail: jsilvest@co.gloucester.nj.us

City Offices
Bernidine Jacobs, Director
Livingston Consumer Affairs
357 South Livingston Avenue
Livingston, NJ 07039
973-535-7976
Fax: 973-740-9408

Maywood Consumer Affairs
Bourough of Maywood
Maywood, NJ 07607
201-845-5749
201-845-5749

Genevieve Ross, Director
Middlesex Borough Consumer Affairs
1200 Mountain Avenue
Middlesex, NJ 08846
732-356-8090, ext. 250
Fax: 732-356-7954

Mildred Pastore, Director
Mountainside Consumer Affairs
1455 Coles Avenue
Mountainside, NJ 07092
908-232-6600

Director Consumer Affairs
Township of North Bergen
4233 Kennedy Blvd.
North Bergen, NJ 07047
201-392-2157 (community service)
201-330-7291 (consumer protection)
Fax: 201-392-8551

Nutley Consumer Affairs
Public Affairs Building
149 Chestnut Street
Nutley, NJ 07110
973-284-4975
Fax: 973-661-9411

Maria Sierra, Consumer Affairs Investigator
Perth Amboy Consumer Affairs
Office of Social Services
Fayette and Read Streets
Perth Amboy, NJ 08861
732-826-4300
Fax: 908-826-6192

Rick Allen Smiley, Director
Plainfield Action Services
City Hall Annex
510 Watchung Avenue
Plainfield, NJ 07060
908-753-3519
Fax: 908-753-3540

Anthony Ioconno, Town Attorney
Secaucus Department of Consumer Affairs
Municipal Government Center
1203 Patterson Plank Road
Secaucus, NJ 07094
201-330-2008

Consumer Affairs Office
1976 Morris Avenue
Union, NJ 07083
908-851-5458
908-851-8501

Charles A. Stern, Director
Wayne Township Consumer Affairs
475 Valley Road
Wayne, NJ 07470
201-694-1800, ext. 3290 201-694-1800,
   ext. 3290

John Weitzel, Director
Weehawken Consumer Affairs
400 Park Avenue
Weehawken, NJ 07087
201-319-6005
Fax: 201-319-0112

Woodbridge Consumer Affairs
Woodbridge Township
One Main Street
Woodbridge, NJ 07095
732-602-6058
Fax: 732-602-6016

NEW MEXICO
State Offices
Consumer Protection Division
Office of the Attorney General
407 Galisteo
Santa Fe, NM 87504-1508
505-827-6060
Toll free in NM: 1-800-678-1508
Fax: 505-827-6685
Web site: www.ago.state.nm.us

NEW YORK
State Offices
Thomas G. Conway, Bureau Chief
Bureau of Consumer Frauds and Protection
Office of the Attorney General
State Capitol
Albany, NY 12224
518-474-5481
Toll free in NY: 1-800-771-7755 (hotline)
Fax: 518-474-3618
Web site: www.oag.state.ny.us

C. Adrienne Rhodes, Chairwoman and
Executive Director
New York State Consumer Protection Board
5 Empire State Plaza
Suite 2101
Albany, NY 12223-1556
518-474-3514
518-474-8583 (capitol region)
Toll free: 1-800-697-1220
Fax: 518-474-2474
E-mail: donna.ned@consumer.state.ny.us
Web site: www.consumer.state.ny.us

Dianne Dixon, Deputy Bureau Chief
Consumer Frauds and Protection Bureau
Office of the Attorney General
120 Broadway, 3rd FL
New York, NY 10271
212-416-8300
Toll free: 1-800-771-7755
Fax: 212-416-6003

Guy Mitchell, Assistant Attorney General in
   Charge
Consumer Fraud and Protection Bureau
New York State Office of the Attorney General
Harlem Regional Office
163 West 125th Street
New York, NY 10027-8201
212-961-4475
Fax: 212-961-4003

Robert Glennon, Assistant Attorney General in Charge
Plattsburgh Regional Office
Office of Attorney General
70 Clinton Street
Plattsburgh, NY 12901
518-562-3282
Fax: 518-562-3294

Gary Brown, Assistant Attorney General in Charge
Consumer Fraud and Protection Bureau
New York State Office of the Attorney General
Westchester Regional Office
101 East Post Road
White Plains, NY 10601-5008
914-422-8755
Fax: 914-422-8706
Regional Offices

Dennis McCabe, Assistant Attorney General
Binghamton Regional Office
New York State Office of the Attorney General
State Office Building, 17th Floor
44 Hawley Street
Binghamton, NY 13901-4433
607-721-8771
Toll free: 1-800-771-7755
Fax: 607-721-8789
E-mail: dennis.mccabe@oag.state.ny.us
Web site: www.oag.state.ny.us

Brooklyn Regional Office
New York State Office of the Attorney General
Consumer Fraud Bureau
55 Hanson Place, Room 732
Brooklyn, NY 11217
718-722-3949
Fax: 718-722-3951

Barbara Kavanaugh, Assistant Attorney General in Charge
Buffalo Regional Office
New York State Office of the Attorney General
Statler Towers
107 Delaware Avenue, 4th Floor
Buffalo, NY 14202
716-853-6271
Toll free: 1-800-771-7755
Fax: 716-853-8414 (Mrs. Smith)

Denis McElligott, Assistant Attorney General in Charge
Suffolk Regional Office
Office of the Attorney General
300 Motor Parkway, Suite 205
Hauppauge, NY 11788
516-231-2401
Fax: 516-435-4757

Poughkeepsie Regional Office
New York State Office of the Attorney General
Poughkeepsie, NY 12601
914-485-3920
Toll free: 1-800-771-7755
TDD/TTY Toll free: 1-800-788-9898
Fax: 914-452-3303
Web site: www.oag.state.ny.us

Marian Payson, Asst. Attorney General in Charge
Rochester Regional Office
Office of the Attorney General
144 Exchange Blvd., 2nd Floor
Rochester, NY 14614
716-546-7430
Toll free: 1-800-771-7755
TDD: 716-327-3249
Fax: 716-546-7514
E-mail: marian.payson@oag.state.ny.us
Web site: www.oag.state.ny.us

Winthrop Thurlow, Assistant Attorney General in Charge
Syracuse Regional Office
Office of the Attorney General
615 Erie Blvd. West, Suite 102
Syracuse, NY 13204-2465
315-448-4848
Fax: 315-448-4851

Joel Marmalstein, Asst. Attorney General in Charge
Utica Regional Office
Office of the Attorney General
207 Genesee Street, Room 504
Utica, NY 13501
315-793-2225
Toll free: 1-800-771-7755
Fax: 315-793-2228
Web site: www.oag.state.ny.us

Office of the Attorney General
Watertown Regional Office
317 Washing Street
Watertown, NY 13601
315-785-2444
Toll free: 1-800-771-7755
Fax: 315-785-2294
Web site: www.oag.state.ny.us

County Offices
Department of Consumer Affairs
Albany County Courthouse
#40
Albany, NY 12207
518-487-5040
Fax: 518-487-5048
E-mail: jmcmahon@albanycounty.com
Web site: www.albanycounty.com

Barbra Kavanaugh, Assistant District Attorney
  in Charge
Consumer Fraud Bureau
Erie County District Attorney's Office
Statler Towers
107 Delaware Ave, 4th Floor
Buffalo, NY 14202
716-853-8404
Toll free in NY: 1-800-771-7755
Fax: 716-853-8414

Charles Gardner, Director
Suffolk County Executive's Office of
  Consumer Affairs
North County Complex, Bldg. 340
Veterans Memorial Highway
Hauppauge, NY 11788
516-853-4600
Fax: 516-853-4825

Jon Van Vlack, Consumer Affairs Director
Ulster County District Attorney's Consumer
  Fraud Bureau
20 Lucas Avenue
Kingston, NY 12401
914-340-3260

Nassau County Office of Consumer Affairs
160 Old Country Road
Mineola, NY 11501
516-571-2600

James Farkas, Director
Rockland County Office of Consumer
  Protection
50 Sanatorium Road
Building P
Pomona, NY 10970
914-364-2681
Fax: 914-364-2694

Dutchess County Department of Consumer
  Affairs
94-A Peach Road
Poughkeepsie, NY 12601
914-486-2949
Fax: 914-486-2947

Douglas Briggs, Director
Schenectady County Consumer Affairs
64 Kellar Avenue
Schenectady, NY 12307
518-356-6795
518-356-7473
Fax: 518-357-0319

Frank Castaldi, Jr., Chief, Economic Crimes
  Bureau
Westchester County District Attorney's Office
111 Martin Luther King Jr. Boulevard
County Courthouse
White Plains, NY 10601
914-285-3303
Fax: 914-285-3594

Frank Castaldi, Jr., Chief
Frauds Bureau
Westchester County District Attorney's Office
111 Grove Street
White Plains, NY 10601
914-285-3414
Fax: 914-285-3594

Elaine Price, Director
Westchester County
Department of Consumer Protection
112 East Post Road
4th Floor
White Plains, NY 10601
914-285-2162
Fax: 914-285-3115
E-mail: epp4@co.westchester.ny.us

City Offices
Gini Faikia, Director
Queens Neighborhood Office
New York City Department of Consumer
  Affairs
120-55 Queens Blvd.
Room 301
Kew Gardens, NY 11424
718-286-2990
Fax: 718-286-2997

Stephen Pedone, Commissioner
Mt. Vernon Office of Consumer Protection
City Hall
11th Floor
Mount Vernon, NY 10550
914-665-2433
Fax: 914-665-2496

Jules Polonetsky, Commissioner
New York City Department of Consumer Affairs
42 Broadway
New York, NY 10004
212-487-4444
212-487-4481 (Spanish)
212-487-4488 (Chinese)
TDD: 212-487-4465
Fax: 212-487-4197
Web site:
  www.ci.nyc.ny.us/html/dca/home.html

Town of Colonial Consumer Protection
Memorial Town Hall
Newtonville, NY 12128
518-783-2790

Schenectady Bureau of Consumer Protection
City Hall, Room 204
Jay Street
Schenectady, NY 12305
518-382-5061
Fax: 518-382-5074

New Justice Conflict Resolution Services, Inc.
1153 West Fayette Street, Suite 301
Syracuse, NY 13204
315-471-4676
Fax: 315-475-0769

Stanley Alexander, Director
Office of Consumer Protection
City of Yonkers
87 Nepperhan Avenue
Yonkers, NY 10701
914-377-6808
Fax: 914-377-6811

NORTH CAROLINA
State Offices
Joshua Stein, Senior Deputy Attorney General
Consumer Protection Division
Office of the Attorney General
P.O. Box 629
Raleigh, NC 27602
919-716-6000
Fax: 919-716-6050
Web site: www.jus.state.nc.us/cpframe.htm

NORTH DAKOTA
State Offices
Wayne Stenehjem, Attorney General
Office of the Attorney General
600 East Boulevard Avenue
Department 125
Bismarck, ND 58505-0040
701-328-2210
TTY 800-366-6888
Fax: 701-328-2226
E-mail: ndag@state.nd.us
Web site: www.ag.state.nd.us

Parrell D. Grossman, Director
Consumer Protection and Antitrust Division
Office of the Attorney General
600 East Boulevard Avenue
Department 125
Bismarck, ND 58505-0040
701-328-3404
Toll free in ND: 1-800-472-2600
TTY 800-366-6888
Fax: 701-328-3535
E-mail: cpat@state.nd.us
Web site:
http://www.ag.state.nd.us/ndag/cpat/cpat.html

OHIO
State Offices
Ohio Attorney General's Office
30 East Broad Street
25th Floor
Columbus, OH 43215-3428
614-466-8831
Toll free in OH: 1-800-282-0515
TDD: 614-466-1393
Fax: 614-728-7583
E-mail: consumer@ag.state.oh.us
Web site: www.ag.state.oh.us

Robert Tongren
Ohio Consumers' Counsel
77 South High Street
15th Floor
Columbus, OH 43266-0550
614-466-8574 (outside OH)
Toll free in OH: 1-877-PICK-OCC (1-877-742-5622)
E-mail: occ@occ.state.oh.us
Web site: www.state.oh.us/cons/

County Offices
Maureen Callahan, Prosecuting Attorney
Summit County Office of Prosecuting Attorney
53 University Avenue
Akron, OH 44308-1680
330-643-2800
TDD/TTY: 330-643-8277 (criminal)
Fax: 330-643-2137 (civil)

Economic Crime
Franklin County Office of Prosecuting Attorney
369 South High Street
Columbus, OH 43215
614-462-3555
Fax: 614-462-6103

Portage County Office of Prosecuting Attorney
466 South Chestnut Street
Ravenna, OH 44266-3000
330-296-4593
Fax: 330-297-3856

City Offices
Department of Neighborhood Services
Cincinnati Office of Consumer Services
801 Plum Street
Cincinnati, OH 45202
513-352-3971
Fax: 513-352-5241

OKLAHOMA
State Offices
Oklahoma Attorney General
Consumer Protection Unit
4545 N. Lincoln Avenue
Suite 260
Oklahoma City, OK 73105
405-521-2029
Toll free: 1-800-448-4904
Fax: 405-528-1867
Web site: www.oag.state.ok.us

Department of Consumer Credit
4545 North Lincoln Blvd., #104
Oklahoma City, OK 73105
405-521-3653
Fax: 405-521-6740

Consumer Protection Division
Office of the Attorney General
440 South Houston, Suite 505
Tulsa, OK 74127-8913
918-581-2885
Fax: 918-581-2917
Web site: www.oag.state.ok.us

OREGON
State Offices
Cheryl Pellegrini, Attorney in Charge
Financial Fraud/ Consumer Protection Section
Department of Justice
1162 Court Street, NE
Salem, OR 97310
503-378-4732
503-378-4320 (hotline Salem only)
503-229-5576 (hotline Portland only)
Toll free in OR: 1-877-877-9392
TDD/TTY: 503-378-5939
Fax: 503-378-5017
Web site: www.doj.state.or.us

PENNSYLVANIA
State Offices
Larry Otter, Senior Deputy Attorney General
　Health Care Unit
Bureau of Consumer Protection
Office of the Attorney General
14th Floor Strawberry Square
Harrisburg, PA 17120
717-705-6938
Toll free in PA: 1-877-888-4877
Fax: 717-787-1190

Frank Donaghue, Director
Bureau of Consumer Protection
Office of Attorney General
14th Floor, Strawberry Square
Harrisburg, PA 17120
717-787-9707
Toll free in PA: 1-800-441-2555
Fax: 717-787-1190
Web site: www.attorneygeneral.gov

Irwin Popowsky, Consumer Advocate
Office of the Consumer Advocate
Office of the Attorney General
Forum Place, 5th Floor
Harrisburg, PA 17101-1921
717-783-5048 (utilities only)
Toll free in PA: 1-800-684-6560
Fax: 717-783-7152
E-mail: paoca@ptd.net
Web site: www.oca.state.pa.us

Regional Offices
Michael Butler, Deputy Attorney General
Bureau of Consumer Protection
Allentown Regional Office
Office of Attorney General
810 Hamilton Street
Fourth Floor
Allentown, PA 18101
610-821-6690
Fax: 610-821-6529

E. Barry Creany, Senior Deputy Attorney
  General
Bureau of Consumer Protection
Ebensburg Regional Office
Office of the Attorney General
171 Lovell Avenue
Suite 202
Ebensburg, PA 15931
814-471-1831
Fax: 814-471-1840

Darrel Vandevald, Deputy Attorney General
Bureau of Consumer Protection
Erie Regional Office
Office of the Attorney General
1001 State Street
Suite 1009
Erie, PA 16501
814-871-4371
Fax: 814-871-4848

Michael Farnan, Deputy Attorney General
Bureau of Consumer Protection
Harrisburg Regional Office
Office of the Attorney General
301 Chestnut Street, Suite 105
Harrisburg, PA 17101
717-787-7109
Fax: 717-772-3560

John Abel, Senior Deputy Attorney General
Bureau of Consumer Protection
Philadelphia Regional Office
Office of the Attorney General
21 South 12th Street
Second Floor
Philadelphia, PA 19107
215-560-2414
Fax: 215-560-2494

Marcia Telek DePaula, Deputy Attorney General
Bureau of Consumer Protection
Pittsburgh Regional office
Office of Attorney General
564 Forbes Avenue
6th Floor Manor Building
Pittsburgh, PA 15219
412-565-5135
Fax: 412-565-5475

J.P. McGowan, Senior Deputy Attorney General
Bureau of Consumer Protection
Scranton Regional Office
Office of Attorney General
214 Samter Building
101 Penn Avenue
Scranton, PA 18503
570-963-4913
Fax: 570-963-3418

County Offices
Beaver County Alliance for Consumer
Protection
699 Fifth Street
Beaver, PA 15009-1997
724-728-7267
Fax: 724-728-6762

A. Courtney Yelle, Director/Chief Sealer
Bucks County Consumer Protection, Weights
  and Measures
50 North Main Street
Doylestown, PA 18901
215-348-7442
Fax: 215-348-4570

Delaware County Consumer Affairs
201 West Front Street
Delaware County Courthouse
Media, PA 19063
610-891-4865
Fax: 610-566-3947

Montgomery County Consumer Affairs
Montgomery County Human Services Center
1430 DeKalb Street
Norristown, PA 19404-0311
610-278-3565
Fax: 610-278-5228

Bruce Sagel, Chief
Economic Crime Unit
Philadelphia District Attorney's Office
1421 Arch Street
Philadelphia, PA 19102
215-686-8750
Fax: 215-686-8765

PUERTO RICO
Puerto Rico Offices
Angel E. Rotger, Secretary
Department of Justice
P.O. Box 902192
San Juan, PR 00902
787-721-2900
Fax: 787-725-2475

Jose Antonio Alicia Rivera, Secretary
Department of Consumer Affairs
Minillas Station
P.O. Box 41059
Santurce, PR 00940-1059
787-721-0940
Fax: 787-726-6570
E-mail: Jalicea@Caribe.net

RHODE ISLAND
State Offices
Vivian Spencer, Director
Consumer Unit
Consumer Protection Unit
Department of Attorney General
150 South Main Street
Providence, RI 02903
401-274-4400
Toll free in RI: 1-800-852-7776
Senior Line: 1-888-621-1112
TDD: 401-453-0410
Fax: 401-222-5110

Mel Stiller, CO-CEO with Bev Tuttle
Consumer Credit Couseling Services
535 Centerville Road
Suite 103
Warwick, RI 02886
Toll free: 1-800-208-2227
Fax: 401-732-0250
Web site: www.creditcounseling.org

SOUTH CAROLINA
State Offices
Evelyn T. Williams, State Ombudsman
Office of Executive Policy and Program
1205 Pendleton Street
Room 308
Columbia, SC 29201
803-734-0457
Toll free in SC only: 1-800-686-0040
Fax: 803-734-0546
Web site: www.state.sc.us

Haviard Jones, Senior Assistant Attorney General
Office of the Attorney General
P.O. Box 11549
Columbia, SC 29211
803-734-3970
Fax: 803-734-4323
Web site: www.scattorneygeneral.org

SC Department of Consumer Affairs
2801 Devine Street
P.O. Box 5757
Columbia, SC 29205-5757
803-734-4200
Toll free in SC: 1-800-922-1594
Fax: 803-734-4286
E-mail: scdca@infoave.net
Web site: www.state.sc.us/consumer

SOUTH DAKOTA
State Offices
Office of the Attorney General
500 East Capitol
State Capitol Building
Pierre, SD 57501-5070
605-773-4400
Toll free in SD: 1-800-300-1986
TDD: 605-773-6585
Fax: 605-773-7163

TENNESSEE
State Offices
Cynthia Kinser, Deputy Attorney General
Division of Consumer Protection
Tennessee Attorney General
425 Fifth Avenue North, 2nd Floor
Nashville, TN 37243-0491
615-741-1671
Fax: 615-532-2910

Mark Williams, Director
Division of Consumer Affairs
5th Floor
500 James Robertson Parkway
Nashville, TN 37243-0600
615-741-4737
Toll free in TN: 1-800-342-8385
Fax: 615-532-4994
E-mail: mwilliams2@mail.state.tn.us
Web site: www.state.tn.us/consumer

TEXAS
State Offices
Paul Elliott, Assistant Attorney General and
  Chief
Consumer Protection Division
Office of Attorney General
P.O. Box 12548
Austin, TX 78711-2548
512-463-2070
Fax: 512-463-8301

Office of Public Insurance Counsel
333 Guadalupe
Suite 3-120
Austin, TX 78701
512-322-4143
Fax: 512-322-4148
E-mail: rod.bordelon@mail.capnet.state.tx.us
Web site: www.opic.state.tx.us

Esther Chavez, Assistant Attorney General
Consumer Protection/ Austin Regional Office
P.O. Box 12548
Austin, TX 78711-2548
512-463-2185
Fax: 512-463-8301
Web site: www.oag.state.tx.us

Consumer Protection/Houston Regional Office
Office of the Attorney General
Houston, TX 77002
713-223-5886, ext. 118
Fax: 713-223-5821
E-mail: john.owens@oag.state.tx.us

Regional Offices
Joyce Iliya, Assistant Attorney General
Consumer Protection Division/Dallas Regional
  Office
Office of the Attorney General
1600 Pacific Avenue, Suite 1700
Dallas, TX 75201-3513
214-969-5310
Fax: 214-969-7615

Consumer Protection/El Paso Regional Office
Office of the Attorney General
El Paso, TX 79901
915-834-5800
E-mail: jad2@oag.state.tx.us

Luke Jordan, Assistant Attorney General
Consumer Protection/Lubbock Regional Office
Office of the Attorney General
916 Main Street, Suite 806
Lubbock, TX 79401-3410
806-747-5238
Fax: 806-747-6307
E-mail: lwj@aog.state.tx.us
Web site: www.oag.state.tx.us

Ric Madrigal, Assistant Attorney General
Consumer Protection/McAllen Regional Office
Office of the Attorney General
3201 North McColl Road, Suite B
McAllen, TX 78501
956-682-4547
Fax: 956-682-1957
Web site: www.oag.state.tx.us

Aaron Valenzuela, Assistant Attorney General
Consumer Protection/San Antonio Regional
  Office
Office of the Attorney General
115 East Travis Street, Suite 925
San Antonio, TX 78205-1615
210-224-1007
Fax: 210-225-1075

County Offices
Beverly Weaver, Director
Department of Environmental and Health
  Services
City Hall
1500 Marilla, Room 7A-North
Dallas, TX 75201
214-670-5216
Fax: 214-670-3863
E-mail: bweaver@gwsmtp.ci.dallas.tx.us

Linda Brown, Director
City of Dallas Economic Development
Department
City Hall
500 Marilla, Room 5C-South
Dallas, TX 75201
214-670-1685
Fax: 214-670-0158
E-mail: lsbrown@ci.dallas.tx.us

Russel Turbeville, Chief
Harris County Consumer Fraud Division
Harris County District Attorney's Office
1201 Franklin
Suite 600
Houston, TX 77002-1901
713-755-5836
713-755-5840
Fax: 713-755-5262

UTAH
State Offices
Francine Giani, Director
Division of Consumer Protection
Department of Commerce
160 East 300 South
Box 146704
Salt Lake City, UT 84114-6704
801-530-6601
Fax: 801-530-6001
E-mail: commerce@br.state.ut.us
Web site: www.commerce.state.ut.us

VERMONT
State Offices
Consumer Assistance Program
For Consumer Complaints & Questions
104 Morrill Hall
UVM
Burlington, VT 05405
802-656-3183 (within Chittenden County or
out of state)
Toll free in VT: 1-800-549-2424
Web site: www.state.vt.us/atg

Henry Marckres, Supervisor
Consumer Assurance Section
Food and Market
Department of Agriculture
116 State Street
Montpelier, VT 05602
802-828-3456
Fax: 802-828-2361

Wendy Morgan, Chief
Public Protection Division
Office of the Attorney General
109 State Street
Montpelier, VT 05609-1001
802-828-5507
Web site: www.state.vt.us/atg

VIRGINIA
State Offices
Andres Alvarez, Program Manager
Office of Consumer Affairs
Department of Agriculture and Consumer
  Services
Washington Building, Suite 100
P.O. Box 1163
Richmond, VA 23219
804-786-2042
Toll free in VA: 1-800-552-9963
TDD: 800-828-1120
Fax: 804-371-7479
Web site: www.vdacs.state.va.us

David B. Irvin, Senior Assistant Attorney
General and Chief
Office of the Attorney General
Antitrust and Consumer Litigation Section
900 East Main Street
Richmond, VA 23219
804-786-2116
Toll free: 1-800-451-1525
Fax: 804-786-0122
E-mail: mail@oag.state.va.us
Web site: www.oag.state.va.us

County Offices
Ardelle Butler, Acting Team Leader
Office of Citizen and Consumer Affairs
#1 Court House Plaza, Suite 310
2100 Clarendon Blvd.
Arlington, VA 22201
703-228-3260
Fax: 703-228-3295
E-mail: abutle@co.arlington.va.us
Web site: www.co.arlington.va.us

Fairfax County Department of
Telecommunications and Consumer Services
12000 Government Center Parkway, Suite 433
Fairfax, VA 22035
703-222-8435
Fax: 703-322-9542

City Offices
Prescott Barbash, Consumer Affairs
Administrator
City of Alexandria
City Hall
P.O. Box 178
Alexandria, VA 22313
703-838-4350
TDD: 703-838-5056
Fax: 703-838-6426
E-mail: prescott.barbash@ci.alexandria.va.us
Web site: ci.alexandria.va.us

Cathy Townsend Parks, Director
Consumer Affairs Division
Office of the Commonwealth's Attorney
2425 Nimmo Pkwy
Virginia Beach, VA 23456-9060
757-426-5836
Fax: 757-427-8779
Web site: www.virginia-
beach.va.us/courts/oca/ca.htm

WASHINGTON
State Offices
Consumer Resource Center
Office of the Attorney General
103 East Holly Street, Suite 308
Bellingham, WA 98225-4728
360-738-6185

Consumer Resource Center
Office of the Attorney General
500 N. Morain Street, Suite 1250
Kennewick, WA 99336-2607
509-734-2967

Consumer Resource Center
Office of the Attorney General
905 Plum Street, Bldg. 3
P.O. Box 40118
Olympia, WA 98504-0118
360-753-6210

Consumer Resource Center
Office of the Attorney General
900 Fourth Avenue, Suite 2000
Seattle, WA 98164-1012
206-464-6684
Toll free in WA: 1-800-551-4636 (Consumer
Resource Centers)
Toll free TDD in WA: 1-800-276-9883
Fax: 206-464-6451
Web site: www.wa.gov/ago

Consumer Resource Center
Office of the Attorney General
1116 West Riverside Avenue
Spokane, WA 99201-1194
509-456-3123

Cynthia Lanphear, Program Manager
Consumer Resource Center
Office of the Attorney General
Consumer Protection Division
1019 Pacific Avenue, 3rd Floor
Tacoma, WA 98402-4411
253-593-2904
Toll free: 1-800-551-4636
Toll free:1-800-276-9883 in state only
Fax: 253-593-2449
E-mail: cynthial@atg.wa.gov
Web site: www.wa.gov/ago

Consumer Resource Center
Office of the Attorney General
1220 Main Street, Suite 510
Vancouver, WA 98660
360-759-2150

City Offices
Revenue and Consumer Affairs
Seattle Department of Finance
Seattle, WA 98134
206-386-1298
Fax: 206-386-1129
E-mail: seattle.consumer-affairs@ci.seattle.wa.us
Web site: www.pan.ci.seattle.wa.us/esd/consumer

Ed Gonzaga, Consumer Affairs Inspector
Revenue and Consumer Affairs Section
Executive Services Department
Division of Finance
600 4th Avenue, #103
Seattle, WA 98104-1891
206-233-7837
Fax: 206-684-5170
E-mail: edgonzaga@ci.seattle.wa.us

Patrick Sainsbury, Chief Deputy Prosecuting
   Attorney
Fraud Division
900 4th Avenue, #1002
Seattle, WA 98164
206-296-9010
Fax: 206-296-9009
E-mail: pat.sainsbury@metrokc.gov
Web site: www.metrokc.gov/proatty/

WEST VIRGINIA
State Offices
Jill Miles, Deputy Attorney General
Consumer Protection Division
Office of the Attorney General
812 Quarrier Street, 6th Floor
P.O. Box 1789
Charleston, WV 25326-1789
304-558-8986
Toll free in WV: 1-800-368-8808
Fax: 304-558-0184
E-mail: consumer@wvnet.edu
Web site: www.state.wv.us/wvag

Karl Angell, Jr., Director
Division of Weights and Measures Section
570 MacCorkle Avenue
St. Albans, WV 25177
304-722-0602
Fax: 304-722-0605
E-mail: angellk@mail.wvnet.edu

WISCONSIN
State Offices
Division of Trade and Consumer Protection
Department of Agriculture
Trade and Consumer Protection
3610 Oakwood Hills Parkway
Eau Claire, WI 54701-7754
715-839-3848
Toll free in WI: 1-800-422-7128
Fax: 715-839-1645

Judy Cardin, Regional Supervisor
Wisconsin Department of Agriculture Trade &
   Consumer Protection
200 North Jefferson Street
Suite 146-A
Green Bay, WI 54301
920-448-5111
920-448-5114
Toll free in WI: 1-800-422-7128
Fax: 920-448-5118
Web site: www.badger.state.wi.us/agencies/datcp

William Oemichen, Administrator
Division of Trade and Consumer Protection
Department of Agriculture
2811 Agriculture Dr.
P.O. Box 8911
Madison, WI 53708
608-224-4953
Toll free in WI: 1-800-422-7128
TTD/TTY: 1-608-224-5058
Fax: 608-224-4939
E-mail: datephotline@wheel.datep.state.wi.us
Web site: www.datcp.state.wi.us

County Offices
Consumer Fraud Unit
Milwaukee County District Attorney's Office
Milwaukee, WI 53233-2485
414-278-4585
Fax: 414-223-1955

Thomas Bauer, Consumer Fraud Investigator
Racine County Sheriff's Department
717 Wisconsin Avenue
Racine, WI 53403
262-636-3126
Fax: 626-637-5279

WYOMING
State Offices
Christopher Petrie, Assistant Attorney General
Office of the Attorney General
Consumer Protection Unit
123 State Capitol Building
Cheyenne, WY 82002
307-777-7874
Toll free in WY only: 1-800-438-5799
Fax: 307-777-7956
E-mail: cpetri@state.wy.us
Web site: www.state.wy.us/~ag/consumer.htm

Other National Consumer Law Center Publications

The National Consumer Law Center publications listed below are in two categories. The first group are books for consumers and counselors. The second group of books are designed primarily for attorneys. More information on all of these books can be found at www.consumerlaw.org or by contacting Publications, National Consumer Law Center, 77 Summer Street, 10th Floor, Boston MA 02110, (617) 542-9595, publications@nclc.org. The books for consumers can be ordered using the form on page 123.

BOOKS FOR CONSUMERS

The National Consumer Law Center Guide to Surviving Debt (2002): Everything a consumer or counselor needs to know about debt collectors, managing credit card debt, whether to refinance, credit card problems, home foreclosures, evictions, repossessions, credit reporting, utility terminations, student loans, budgeting, and bankruptcy.

The National Consumer Law Center Guide to Consumer Rights for Immigrants (2002): Key information on notario and immigration consultant fraud, money wire transfers, credit reporting, affidavits of support, cashing checks and opening bank accounts, used car fraud, telephone service, student loans and much more.

Return to Sender: Getting a Refund or Replacement for Your Lemon Car (2000): How lemon laws work, what consumers and their lawyers should know to evaluate each other, how to develop the facts, legal rights, and how to handle both informal dispute resolution proceedings, and more.

BOOKS FOR LAWYERS

The Consumer Credit and Sales Legal Practice Series contains 16 titles, each with a CD-Rom that allows users to copy information directly onto a word processor. Each manual is designed to be an attorney's primary practice guide and legal resource when representing clients in all fifty states on that consumer law topic, and is updated annually. The 16 titles are arranged into four "libraries":

DEBTOR RIGHTS LIBRARY

Consumer Bankruptcy Law and Practice: The definitive personal bankruptcy manual with step-by-step instructions from initial interview to final discharge and including consumers' rights as creditors when a merchant or landlord files for bankruptcy. Appendices and CD-Rom contain over 130 annotated pleadings, bankruptcy statutes, rules and fee schedules, an interview questionnaire, a client handout, and software to complete petitions and schedules.
2000 Sixth Edition, 2001 Supplement, and 2001 CD-Rom, Including Law Disk's Bankruptcy Forms

Fair Debt Collection: The basic reference in the field, covering the Fair Debt Collection Practices Act and common law, state statutory and other federal debt collection protections. Appendices and companion CD-Rom contain numerous practice aids, including sample pleadings and discovery materials, the FDCPA, the FTC's Official Staff Commentary, *all* FTC staff opinion letters, and summaries of reported and unreported cases.
2000 Fourth Edition, 2001 Supplement, and 2001 CD-Rom

Repossessions (and Foreclosures): Unique guide to home foreclosures, car and mobile home repossessions, threatened seizures of household goods, tax and other statutory liens, and default remedies relating to automobile leases and rent-to-own transactions. Appendices and CD-Rom reprint relevant UCC provisions and comments, summarize all state foreclosure and right-to-cure laws, and present various sample pleadings.
1999 Fourth Edition, 2001 Cumulative Supplement, and 2001 CD-Rom

Student Loan Law: Student loan debt collection and collection fees; discharges based on closed school, false certification, failure to refund, disability, and bankruptcy; tax intercepts, wage garnishment, and offset of social security benefits; repayment plans, consolidation loans, and deferments, and non-payment of loan based on school fraud. CD-Rom and appendices contain numerous forms, pleadings, interpretation letters and regulations.
2001 First Edition with CD-Rom

Access to Utility Service: The only examination of consumer rights when dealing with regulated, de-regulated, and unregulated utilities, covering electric, gas, oil, propane, and other fuels, and telecommunications. Everything from terminations and billing errors to low-income payment plans, fuel allowances in subsidized housing, LIHEAP, and weatherization. Includes summaries of state utility regulations, key statutes and regulations.
2001 Second Edition with CD-Rom

CREDIT AND BANKING LIBRARY

Truth in Lending: Detailed analysis of *all* aspects of TILA, the Consumer Leasing Act, and the Home Ownership and Equity Protection Act. Appendices and the CD-Rom contain the Acts, Reg. Z, Reg. M, and their Official Staff Commentaries, sample pleadings and rescission notice, and a program to compute APRs.
1999 Fourth Edition, 2001 Cumulative Supplement, and 2001 CD-Rom with APR Program

Fair Credit Reporting Act: The key resource for handling any type of credit reporting issue, from cleaning up blemished credit records to obtaining credit despite negative information to suing reporting agencies and creditors for inaccurate reports. Covers the FCRA, the Credit Repair Organizations Act, state credit reporting and repair statutes and common law claims.
1998 Fourth Edition, 2001 Cumulative Supplement, and 2001 CD-Rom

Consumer Banking and Payments Law: Unique analysis of consumer law as to checks, money orders, and international wires; credit, debit, ATM, and stored value cards; banker's right of set off; electronic transfer of food stamps and other state benefits, direct deposits of federal payments, and other electronic transfers. The CD-Rom and appendices reprint relevant statutes, regulations, and interpretations.
2001 First Edition with CD-Rom

The Cost of Credit: Regulation and Legal Challenges: A one-of-a-kind resource detailing state and federal regulation of consumer credit in all fifty states, federal usury preemption, explaining credit math, and how to challenge excessive credit charges and credit insurance. The CD-Rom includes a credit math program and hard-to-find agency interpretations.
2000 Second Edition, 2001 Supplement, and 2001 CD-Rom

Credit Discrimination: Analysis of the Equal Credit Opportunity Act, Fair Housing Act, Civil Rights Acts, and state statutes concerning discrimination in mortgages and other credit transactions, including reprints of federal statutes, FRB Reg. B and Commentary, HUD fair housing regulations, sample pleadings, and consent agreements.
1998 Second Edition, 2001 Cumulative Supplement, and 2001 CD-Rom

CONSUMER LITIGATION LIBRARY

Consumer Arbitration Agreements: Numerous approaches to challenge the enforceability of a binding arbitration agreement, the interrelation of the Federal Arbitration Act and state law, class actions in arbitration, the right to discovery, and other topics. Appendices and CD-Rom include sample discovery, numerous briefs, and the rules of the two major arbitration mechanisms.
2001 First Edition with CD-Rom

Consumer Class Actions: A Practical Litigation Guide: Makes class action litigation manageable even for small offices, including numerous sample pleadings, class certification memoranda, discovery, class notices and settlement materials.
1999 Fourth Edition and 1999 CD-Rom

Consumer Law Pleadings on CD-Rom: Over 600 notable recent pleadings from all types of consumer cases — home foreclosures, landlord-tenant, mobile homes, car cases, debt collection, fair credit reporting, home improvement fraud, flipping, yield spread premiums, fringe lending, rent to own, student loans, mandatory arbitration clauses, force-placed insurance, lender liability, and many others. Special finding aids pinpoint the desired pleading in seconds, ready to paste into a word processing program.
2001 CD-Rom with Index Guide: ALL pleadings from ALL NCLC Manuals, including Consumer Law Pleadings Numbers One through Seven

DECEPTION AND WARRANTIES LIBRARY

Unfair and Deceptive Acts and Practices: The only practice manual covering all aspects of a deceptive practices case in every state. Special sections on automobile sales, the federal racketeering (RICO) statute, unfair insurance practices, and the FTC Holder Rule.
2001 Fifth Edition with 2001 CD-Rom

Automobile Fraud: Detailed examination of odometer tampering, lemon laundering, sale of salvage, wrecked, and flood-damaged cars, undisclosed damage to new cars, and deception as to prior use, litigating fraud claims for punitive damages, numerous sample pleadings, and investigating a car's prior history, including state procedures for title searches.
1998 First Edition, 2001 Cumulative Supplement, and 2001 CD-Rom

Consumer Warranty Law: Comprehensive treatment of state new and used car lemon laws, the federal Magnuson-Moss Warranty Act, UCC Articles 2 and 2A, mobile home warranty legislation, new home warranty law, FTC Used Car Rule, negligence and strict liability theories, car repair and home improvement statutes, service contract and lease laws. Also includes sample pleadings and discovery, notice of revocation, and other practice aids.
2001 Second Edition with CD-Rom

NCLC'S CD-ROMS

Every NCLC manual is accompanied with a cumulative CD-Rom. Users need only have one CD-Rom per manual. NCLC's CD-Roms feature pop-up menus for easy use, PDF format with Internet-style navigation, the full text of manual appendices, indices, and contents, many pleadings and hard-to-find agency interpretations and legislative history not included in the manual appendices, and other invaluable practice aids. Documents can be copied into a word processing program. Of special note is NCLC's *Consumer Law in a Box:*

Consumer Law in a Box: a CD-Rom combining all documents and software from 16 other NCLC CD-Roms. Allows one to quickly pinpoint the correct document from thousands found on the CD through key word searches and Internet-style navigation, links, bookmarks, and other finding aids. Includes two credit math programs and bankruptcy software. *December 2001 CD-Rom*

OTHER NCLC PUBLICATIONS FOR LAWYERS

NCLC REPORTS: A newsletter covering the latest developments and ideas in the practice of consumer law. *Issued 24 times a year*

STOP Predatory Lending: A Guide for Legal Advocates: Provides a roadmap and practical legal strategy and resources on litigating the range of predatory lending abuse from small loans to abusive mortgage loans. The CD-Rom contains a credit math program, pleadings, legislative and administrative materials, and underwriting guidelines. *2002 First Edition with CD-Rom*

Sourcebook of the Annual National Consumer Rights Litigation Conference: Once a year, the nation's top consumer law practitioners share what works for them, with practical advice, sample pleadings, new legal developments, novel theories, and key cases. *October 2001 Edition with Disk*

ORDER FORM

☐ The NCLC Guide to Surviving Debt (2002 ed.) ....$19 ppd.

☐ The NCLC Guide to Consumer Rights for Immigrants
(2002 ed.)...$10 ppd.

☐ The NCLC Guide to Mobile Homes (2002 ed.)....................$12 ppd.

☐ Return to Sender: Getting a Refund or Replacement for Your
Lemon Car (2000 ed.) ....$16 ppd.

☐ Please send me more information about NCLC books for lawyers.

Name _____

Organization_____

Street Address _____

City _____ State _____ Zip _____

Telephone_____

Fax _____

E-mail_____

Mail to: National Consumer Law Center, Inc.
Publications Department
77 Summer Street, 10th Floor
Boston, MA 02110-1006

| **Telephone orders** |
| (617) 542-9595 |
| or fax (617) 542-8028 |
| for credit card orders |

☐ Check or money order enclosed, payable
to the National Consumer Law Center

☐ MasterCard   ☐ VISA

Card# ☐☐☐☐☐☐☐☐☐☐☐☐☐☐☐☐☐

Exp. date ☐☐☐☐ Signature _____

(card number, expiration date, and signature must accompany charge orders)

NATIONAL CONSUMER LAW CENTER
77 Summer Street, 10th Floor • Boston, MA 02110-1006
Tel. (617) 542-9595 • FAX (617) 542-8028 • publications@nclc.org

www.consumerlaw.org

Glossary

Camber. Slightly convex arch, which is built into a load bearing beam, truss or girder designed to counteract any load bearing stress place on it.

Cap, Block. Often called a paving block, this thin, flat piece of masonry is used to cap off a wall.

Crawl Space. Space between the ground and the first floor of a home, which allows for access to wiring, plumbing, etc., approximately four feet.

Crown. Outward bowing of a board or the high point of joists, rafters, and other framing members.

Eaves. That part of a roof that extends beyond the sidewall forming an overhang. Eaves are comprised of a fascia, soffit and soffit molding.

HUD (U.S. Department of Housing and Urban Development). Federal agency overseeing the Federal Housing Administration and other housing and community development programs.

I-beam. Structural steel beam, called an I-beam because cross-section looks like the capital letter "I". I-beams are used for support with long spans.

Jamb. The sides, top, and bottom of window and door frames.

Joist. Horizontal, parallel beams that provide support for the boards of a floor or the laths of a ceiling.

Mobile Home. Pre-manufactured structure that is designed to be transported to a site and semi-permanently attached there.

Modular Housing. Dwelling units constructed from components prefabricated in a factory and erected on the site.

Pier. Column designed to support a concentrated load. Pier columns are made of steel, steel reinforced concrete or wood.

Racking. Occurs when a force causes a structure to shift so that it is out of plumb.

Rafter. A sloping structural member running from the ridge of a roof to the eaves that supports the roof sheathing and covering.

Rake. A roof overhang on a building's gable end.

Ridge Board. Horizontal board that serves as a support in the highest point of the roof structure and into which the upper ends of rafters are fastened.

R-Value. Measurement of a material's resistance to heat loss, most often referring to insulation products. The higher the R-Value, the slower the rate of loss.

Sheathing. Boards or sheet material that are fastened to roofs and exterior walls and on which the roof covering and siding are applied.

Site Built Home. A home that is constructed "on site" on a piece of property chosen by the potential homeowner.

Skirt. Siding that covers the area from the base to the ground of a mobile home or porch.

Soffit. Underside trim member of the roof overhang.

Soffit Vent. Vent opening in the soffit of a building used for ventilation and to allow heat to escape from the attic.

Studs. Upright pieces of lumber or steel in a wall to which coverings such as drywall, siding or other types of panels are attached.

Truss. An engineered assembly of wood or wood and metal members used to support roofs or floors.

Vapor Barrier. Material that prevents the passage of moisture.

Wind Load or Force. Effect on a structure caused by the force of the wind blowing on it, which is considered during the design phase.

Index